Let The Tooth Be Known

Written and Illustrated by
Dawn Ewing, RDH, PhD, ND
Doctor of Integrative Medicine

Cover design by Curtiss Lanham

Copyright 1998 by Dawn Ewing
Revised 2nd Edition 2002
Published by Holistic Health Alternatives

ISBN #0-9669404-1-5
Previously ISBN #09669404-0-7

This book is dedicated to
My husband Toby and my children Nikki and Trevor.
Without their love and support I would not be able to
grow and learn.
I thank GOD for my family.

To Bill and Joanne Glaros

For being visionaries and mentors.

Table Of Contents

Forward

By William P. Glaros, DDS

The challenge to a health-conscious person today is tremendous. With the current explosion of health and wellness information, how does a consumer make the best choices for one's self and loved ones? Which of the often conflicting "truths" will work best for a conscientious decision-maker?

Informed people have an information database in areas that are familiar to them, but what about new areas such as *Biological Dentistry*? What is Biological Dentistry? Who does it concern? Where are the sources of facts? How can it be more understandable? Who can best help with the questions about the questions?

Allow me to introduce Dawn Ewing, RDH, ND, Ph.D., Doctor of Integrative Medicine and licensed EMT-P. We have worked together in my office for nine years, as we explore, experiment, and expand our concepts of Biological Dentistry. Dr. Ewing's impressive educational credentials, along with her life as a devoted wife and mother, give her an enlightened and sensitive perspective on the revolutionary field named Biological Dentistry.

This enlightening book is more like a conversation than a text. Dawn's writing style is frank and to the point - just like Dawn. The pages are packed with information that effervesces at its own pace and in its own space - just like Dawn. The purpose is to be helpful and the message is sincere - just like Dawn.

In Dawn Ewing you get a guide to help you sort through the seeming contradictions, a human bridge to narrow the information gaps and personalize the facts available in the printed and the electronic literature. As a reference book or as a cover-to-cover experience, I invite you to enjoy your journey through <u>Let the Tooth Be Known</u>.

William P. Glaros, D.D.S., F.A.G.D.
Fellow of The Academy of General Dentistry
President of The American Academy of Biological Dentistry 2002-2004
Member of The International Academy of Oral Medical Toxicology
Member of The Holistic Dental Association
Member of The Price Pottinger Foundation
Diplomate of Naturopathy granted by the American Naturopathic Association

"Drill - Fill - Bill"

By John Parks Trowbridge, M.D.

This old phrase - "Drill - Fill - Bill" - has been used for years to summarize the practice of dentistry. Unfortunately, the *old* phrase *still* explains most of the practice of many dentists.

Ever since Dr. Morton discovered "laughing gas" as an effective "knock-out" for painful procedures, patients have looked for a "painless dentist" in their town and dentists have looked for the easiest and best ways to fill cavities. Indeed, anyone who has suffered the excruciating pain from an infected tooth looks back on the dentist who rescued him with a fond memory.

But dentistry, unfortunately, has succumbed to a fearful popularity contest, namely how to provide fast, painless, immediate, and effective "fixes" to cavities and to injured teeth without regard to future health consequences. And the results can be severe and damaging. Pause for a minute to realize that the two greatest "public health experiments" of our modern era are the use of fluoride in the water supply and the use of mercury in fillings. Medical studies suggest that these two chemicals are highly toxic and have created (or contributed to) many of the disabling illness' of our time.

Tooth decay - cavities - that's what most of us think of when we think of dentistry. Indeed, tooth decay is more a matter of diet and oral hygiene than anything else. When "native" cultures become "civilized" and begin eating "foods of commerce," tooth decay is one of the first results. Weston Price, one of the most brilliant dentists of the twentieth century, studied cultures around the world and showed that other degenerative diseases quickly follow the change to the "Western diet," high in sugars and starches and in foods that have been processed, preserved, and sent to market. Degenerative diseases such as diabetes, heart disease, hardening of the arteries, even osteoporosis. The very ones that are claiming the comfort and even the lives of our friends, our parents, even ourselves.

To help "prevent" tooth decay, dentists and politicians have exposed *everyone*, without choice, to fluoride-a toxic chemical. To treat cavities -"Drill - Fill - and Bill" - dentists have opted for the "easy way out," using mercury - a highly toxic metal. (In case you don't already know, "silver" fillings are mostly mercury {toxic}, some silver, and a dash of tin {toxic} and zinc along with other metals.) To "preserve" an injured or dead tooth, dentists have adopted another "easy answer" - the root canal procedure, where a hole is drilled down the tooth to the roots and it is stuffed to the brim with mercury and other toxic compounds and then "capped" or "filled." Still other dentists have chosen the more technical use of space age metals as posts to hold teeth in place on the bone.

To "fill in the gaps," dentists have chosen to insert "bridges" where metal fixtures can cross the midline of the mouth (possibly upsetting energy balances for the body). To remove severely damaged teeth, dentists have chosen to yank and chisel, often leaving frayed pieces to later fester and develop deep-seated infection. To replace a mouthful of missing teeth, dentists have chosen "plates" that are loaded with toxic mercury compounds.

When someone visits a dentist, he gets told "your teeth look alright." But what about your jawbone - do you have a festering "cavitation" (hole in the bone), such as might arise

7

after an extraction (even after removal of your "wisdom teeth"). When someone asks about whether "mercury fillings" (which dentists call "silver fillings") are safe to be in their mouth, he gets told a reassuring deception, that "the American Dental Association hasn't found any problems at all, in over a hundred years of use."

This might sound like ranting and raving of an angry patient who was "done wrong" by some dentist in the distant past. Not so. In actual fact, I'm a highly trained physician whose job is to find what's wrong with people who come in to see me after they've been told "you don't have a problem that we can find," or "we don't have any other treatment for your condition," or "you can't be having symptoms like you describe - go to a psychiatrist," or some such malarkey.

Over the years, my job has been to "find what's wrong and fix it." Actually God does all the healing - but I help out by finding what raw materials are missing (nutrition), finding what toxic poisons could be blocking (such as mercury or festering infection), and then finding and "turning on the switch" to start the healing (thyroid, other hormones, oxygen, whatever). And one of my best allies in solving patient problems - with "medical" diseases - has been my friend since 1982, Dr. Bill Glaros, a "biological dentist" and, of late, one of Dr. Dawn Ewing's mentors.

They haven't helped me to solve "dental" problems - they've helped me solve "medical" problems with some sophisticated "dentistry" approaches...."biological dentistry" approaches, that is. Way more than "Drill - Fill - and Bill." And way more successful.

Recent scientific advances have shown disturbing conclusions about how "dental care" (as I outlined above) can make people sick. What's more exciting, though, is that "biological dentistry" can help make people well.

Over the past 15 years, I've watched as the NEW dentistry has taken rediscovered past conclusions (such as those of Dr. Weston Price about root canals and jaw infections) and new discoveries (such as "space age" materials to replace toxic metals) to forge a dramatically better understanding on how to help people recover better health. There are only two gloomy clouds in this picture: first, unfortunately only a few hundred enlightened professionals offer biological dentistry care, and second, many of them have come under vicious attack (by other dentists and by State regulatory boards) for doing nothing more than being successful where "old dentistry" had failed to help.

Dr. Hal Huggins (one of Dr. Glaros' mentors) helped to pioneer this NEW dentistry, insisting that we should put materials into people's mouths that will not set up an immune reaction and that won't otherwise poison the body. Sam Ziff helped to popularize this concept by calling "silver" dental fillings "the toxic bomb." The sad fact is that many patients and dentists will assume that defusing the time bomb involves nothing more than selecting a different compound to stuff into cavities - the same old "Drill - Fill - and Bill" with just a slight twist. But courageous dentists, working with physicians (M.D.'s and D.O.'s) who understand that people really can recover better health, have developed far more sophisticated approaches than are understood by "regular dentists" and "regular doctors."

To keep this limited viewpoint from taking over, Dr. Ewing's book will be an invaluable handbook for patients and dentists alike. She has covered not only the basics but also the emerging methods of diagnosis and advanced treatment. Some patients will do well simply to have their fillings "changed out" (properly, not casually!) with newer, more compatible, less toxic materials. Others will also need removal of root canals and probing of deeper (yet unsuspected) jaw infections. Some will need customized assistance, such as homeopathy, acupuncture, cranio-sacral manipulation, and other aspects of "energy medicine." Many will need chelation therapy, the only available treatment for removing toxic metals in the body - along with herbal detoxification therapies and personalized nutritional support.

Regardless of the complexity of any patient's problem, **Let the Tooth be Known** ... will provide guidance to physicians, dentists, and patients alike. After all, a starting point is always required if you want to take the path to healing. To many patients - who have rightfully felt that the "light at the end of the tunnel" was, indeed, simply an "oncoming train" - Dr. Ewing's book will turn the spotlight into the shadows, showing them for the first time how they got sick and how they can work to get well.

The deep, dark secret in modern dentistry is that people get relief from their immediate pain but get sicker and sicker and sicker because of the toxic metals and chemicals their dentists have poured into their mouths. And because dentists reassure patients that "there's nothing wrong" when, indeed, the answers are there to be found by professionals using the advanced techniques and treatments of the NEW dentistry.

Lest you misunderstand that I'm talking about discomforts and problems in your mouth, let me assure you that I'm talking from the perspective of a "wholistic" physician, taking care of the "whole patient." Ours is an era of devastating diseases that relentlessly claim the comfort and independence of their victims - diseases such as diabetes, heart disease, hardening of the arteries, liver failure, MS (multiple sclerosis), myasthenia gravis, and so on. A startling number of these problems can improve dramatically - beyond a patient's fondest dreams - when enlightened medical and dental practitioners team up to remove toxic metals and chemicals, to remove unsuspected sites of infection, to restore nutritional balance, and to employ advanced techniques of "biological dentistry."

As I finish writing this introduction, I am struck by a strange thought. For as long as I have known about this field, isn't it odd that only now is a comprehensive handbook becoming available. Millions of patients -me, my wife, my children, and countless others though the years - will thank you, Dawn, for making these awareness' available.

John Parks Trowbridge, M.D.
Fellow of the American College for Advancement in Medicine
Diplomate of the American Board of Chelation Therapy
Program Chair, Advanced Seminar in Heavy Metal Toxicity
Past-president, Great Lakes College of Clinical Medicine
Author of :
"The Yeast Syndrome"
"Do What You Want To Do: Get Pain Relief Now"
"Living Well Past 50: Rejuvenate Your Heart and Arteries"

Disclaimer

This book contains information, opinions and conclusions
drawn from my experiences. I cannot be responsible for
adverse effects that may occur from use of the
information contained in this book.

Dr. Dawn Ewing

CHAPTER ONE

THE DENTAL ENVIRONMENT

Most people have heard about recycling and being kind to the environment. Some people have become ill while working in sick buildings and others while living in their own castle (their home). The point I would like to discuss is the environment inside the dental office.

Most people have a *fear* of going to the dentist. "It smells funny", say most patients. "I hate the sound of the drill", says another. Well, what about the employees? They have to be around those smells and sounds. Is it safe? What about the patients? Is it safe for them?

A dental office **is** a hazardous place to work. There are 2,000 plus chemicals, blood bourne pathogens, poor lighting, high pitched sounds and many other environmental issues that need to be addressed.

We will begin with water. The water in the office where I work has a filter that can purify and alkalinize the water. Overnight and on weekends the water standing in the lines of all the drills and water syringes in a dental office, breeds bacteria. ABC NEWS 20/20 did an extensive report on the issue, claiming the water in most dental office lines was dirtier than their toilet water. What about chlorine? Chlorine is a problem for some chemically sensitive patients. We installed a bacterial and chemical filter on <u>every line in each operatory</u> so the water is absolutely clean. This means each room has 4 or 5 filters. The filters are discarded and replaced to ensure clean water is being delivered to the patient. Each filter costs $2.50, so you can see this is not a cheap process. When we had the filters installed, the water lines were filled with bacteria. The filters would only last through one or two patients. We had the filters sent to a lab for testing. We finally had the entire water lines replaced in each room. Knowing what I know now, I must admit that my stomach turns each time I think of all the water squirted into people's mouths to rinse. Does your Dental office have filters? For more information on water filters for dental offices, call 800-524-6984.

Lighting is another issue. Most of our patients come to us because they know we are a safe place to be. Some people are sensitive to fluorescent bulbs. Every bulb in our office is full spectrum, which is healthier. For information on lights go to www.naturallighting.com. We spend a major part of our life in the work environment and need to be healthy to meet the needs of our patients. It is also important to have a lot of natural light, and we do. Each of our operatories has an entire wall that is glass, overlooking an atrium of trees, plants and flowers.

There are safety glasses for the patient to wear; this prevents any damage to the eye from debris during the clinical procedures. Does your dentist provide you with protective eyewear?

What about the sound? Most dentists, hygienists and assistants have hearing problems due to the frequency of the drill. Just think, in order to see, the dentist must have his head very close to your mouth and immediately next to the drill in his hand. The Houston Dental Association sponsored a hearing loss awareness clinic at a dental meeting I attended. The plan was to educate dentists and staff about the need for ear filters. It is like working around a jack hammer all day. I participated in the course that was at the seminar. It was noteworthy that most dentists had high frequency loss from the use of the high speed drill, and most hygienists had low pitch loss from using the slower, low speed drills.

Well, if you aren't scared to work in a dental office yet, just wait. Chemicals and toxins are all over. Most conventional offices use mercury silver to fill cavities. Years ago, I worked in an office that was recarpeted. A ball of mercury was found behind each of the dental units. The process of mixing the mercury with the silver filling used to be done by hand. This meant a little mercury was easy to spill on occasion. Removing a silver filling involves drilling out the old filling. This process creates a high level of mercury vapor. When the mercury vapor is inhaled it stays in the body and accumulates. The dental industry does make some new heavy duty vacuums and filters that go in the room to purify the air. While we are talking about mercury vapors, a new filter has just become available for the suction trap. As a filling is removed and suctioned into the vacuum, it ends up in a trap. This filter would collect the vapors and be disposed of at certain intervals. Measuring the amount of mercury vapor coming out of dental offices has been the subject of several studies. This mercury vapor that vents to the outside world adds to the toxic waste in the environment.

Another source of vapor is from the autoclave or chemiclave. This is the oven used to sterilize instruments at 220 degrees for 20 minutes. Using an autoclave to sterilize instruments prevents passing blood bourne diseases on to other patients. A lot of older model autoclaves use a chemical rather than water to heat and circulate inside the oven. When these autoclaves are opened they vent a gas. This gas cloud is formaldehyde! The cloud of gas makes your eyes burn and tear. There are newer models that use water and eliminate the formaldehyde gas formation. Most dentists don't want to spend the money on a new autoclave if the old one works. In this case, the autoclave should be in a well-vented area and the staff needs to be educated about the hazard involved from breathing the fumes. Does your dentist have an autoclave? Another source of vapors is found when cleaning the tanks of the x-ray processor. When you empty the tank, the instructions tell you to empty one tank at a time. To decrease the amount of time spent standing there; most assistants pull the plug on both tanks at the same time. This allows the chemical vapors to blend together and this is particularly dangerous to any pregnant employee. Gloves and a mask should be worn to prevent as much contact as possible with the chemicals.

We have 2 six inch ring binders filled with Material Safety Data Sheets (MSDS) on every product used in the office. It is mandatory that employees are trained in the use of the books. There are several chemicals that when mixed together, will spontaneously combust if wiped up with a paper towel. Those chemicals must be wiped up with a wet paper towel or a special vermiculite substance. The Material Safety Data Sheets explain each product, its chemical content, what personal protective equipment should be worn, how the product is hazardous, the routes of exposure and how to dispose of a spill. I have spoken with the State Health Department in Texas several times. The first time I spoke with them they put me in touch with a special division because the materials I was requesting information on are so hazardous. The man I spoke with was astonished to find out that these materials were common in dental offices and some were even being placed in people's mouths.

If the office is using laughing gas, it is important to have a scavenger unit on the mask. If this extra equipment is not in place, an incredible amount of gas can be found leaking into the air around the dentist and the assistant. Again, this is a bad place for a woman of child-bearing age to be working.

There are x-rays being taken all day long in the dental office. Is there a lead shield for both the patient and the operator? Is there a lead collimator in the x-ray head? Has the state inspected the x-ray for leaks? Is the film being used the fastest speed available to reduce the exposure time? A biological dentist may provide a homeopathic remedy to help neutralize the negative effects of radiation to the body. New digital x-rays are just becoming available. These machines are

17

expensive but will dramatically reduce x-ray exposure to the patient and the staff.

The Occupational Safety and Health Administration (OSHA) requires the dental staff have a good working knowledge of the risks to blood, saliva and diseases. It wants the employees to know when and what PPE (Personal Protective Equipment) or BSI (Body Substance Isolation) to use. This usually involves the use of gloves, masks, protective eye wear, ear plugs, etc. What happens to the person, either patient or employee, that is allergic to latex? Our office is virtually latex free. There are gloves made of vinyl or nitrile; a supply should be kept for the latex sensitive individual to use. The rubber cups to polish teeth are latex; the biological office will order ones that are non-latex. All products must be labeled clearly so the employee will know how to protect themselves from exposure. For instance, a dental assistant pours a model of plaster of paris. The container that the plaster of paris is in would have a sign explaining the need for gloves, mask and eyewear. It will also give the route of entry i.e.: *Plaster of Paris: Long term exposure to inhalation of dust may cause severe lung damage.*

The office I am in uses music and color to create a loving, calm and healing environment. The music that comes in by satellite is peaceful harp and piano music. There are angels used to decorate and sayings that remind us of God.

I love my office. I feel safe and very comfortable.

Working in an intense environment can be a drain on one's energy. I actually feel that I benefit from the time I spend at the office. By benefit I mean more than just financially. I feel healthier and recharged.

Dental Terminology

Anterior teeth- The cuspids, lateral incisors and central incisors are the front or anterior teeth.

Posterior teeth- The bicuspids and molars, including wisdom teeth.

Maxilla- The upper jaw.

Maxillary teeth- Any tooth on the upper jaw.

Mandible- The lower jaw.

Mandibular- Any tooth on the lower jaw.

TMJ- Temporal Mandibular Joint, the joint or hinge area where the upper and lower jaw connects.

Clinical Crown- The portion of the tooth that is above the gum, visible with the naked eye.

Crown- Also called caps, a dental restoration that covers the entire tooth. These can be made of gold, non-precious metals, non-precious metal with porcelain baked on, or a non-metallic material. This restoration is usually made in a lab and cemented to the tooth later.

Inlay/Onlay-A more conservative dental restoration than a crown because it does not cover the entire tooth. This type of restoration is usually made at a lab. Materials similar to those of a crown are used and this is cemented in place at a second visit.

19

Root Canals- Teeth that have had the nerve and blood supply removed and filled with other materials, like Gutta Percha, Silver Points or Biocalix.

Bitewing x-ray- Used to detect decay in-between the back teeth. Also helpful in evaluating the bone level around the teeth.

Panographic x-ray- Takes an x-ray of the entire mouth by going around the head, useful in diagnosis of osteonecrosis and for viewing third molars.

Periapical X-ray- An x-ray that takes a view of the root of the tooth.

Partial Dentures- Removable teeth that replace 1 or more missing teeth on either the upper or lower jaw without replacing all the teeth.

Full Denture- Replaces all the teeth on the upper or lower jaw.

Night Guard- Also referred to as an occlusal splint, a plastic appliance that covers the teeth to prevent clenching or grinding.

Quadrant- One quarter of the mouth.

Gingiva- The gum tissue.

Occlusal- The chewing surface of a tooth.

Distal- Side of the tooth furthest from the midline of the mouth.

Mesial- Side of the tooth closest to the midline of the mouth.

Lingual- Tongue side of a tooth.

Buccal- Cheek side of a tooth.

Cusp tips- The highest points on the chewing surfaces of teeth.

CHAPTER TWO

BIOENERGETICS

First, we want to get a clear picture of what we are talking about when we use the term Bioenergetics. As defined by the National Institute of Health; Bioenergetics is "*The scientific study of interactions between living organisms and electromagnetic fields, forces, energies, currents and charges.*" Bioenergetics studies the endogenous electromagnetic fields which originate inside the organism, and exogenous ones which originate outside the organism.

INSTRUMENTS USED TO MEASURE BIOENERGY

X-rays, CAT scans, Volt Meters, Thermometers, Magnetoencephalographs, Stethoscopes, Light Meters, Weight Scales, Ohmmeters, Magnetic Resonance Imaging (MRI), Sphygmomanometers, Electrocardiographs (ECG/EKG), Electroencephalographs (EEG) Electromyographs (EMG) and Sound Meters .

Using these devices, you are able to measure temperature, mass, volume, or pressure. This gives information about the chemical, mechanical, magnetic or electrical energy involved. The electrocardiograph (ECG or EKG), the electromyograph (EMG), and the electroencephalogram (EEG) are examples of electronic instruments that receive very small signals and magnify the signal for display.

Electrocardiograph- The ECG also known as an EKG was first developed in 1887. It records the electrical activity from different areas of the heart in a graph form. It illustrates the electrical activity in the heart by displaying the small voltages generated through the heart muscle. We know when we see the p-wave that the electricity started in the atria. By the length of the p-wave we can tell where in the atria it originated. Even with all the information that the EKG gives, it is impossible to determine if the heart is beating. It is possible for the heart to have electrical activity that looks normal and healthy but **not be beating**. This is a condition called Electro Mechanical Disassociation. Can you imagine how ludicrous it must have sounded to physicians to hear about the EKG when it first came out? You put sticky pads on the chest, arms and legs, introduce electricity and you have an image of where the infarcted (dead) tissue is after a myocardial infarction (heart attack). Electrical impulses do not pass through dead tissue. This technology allows the physician to diagnose the damage done to the cardiac muscle. Must have seemed insane when it was first introduced, but years of use prove it works.

Electroencephalograph- The EEG was developed in 1875. It records electrical activity from various areas of the brain. This electrical recording is sensitive to different stimuli. Here is an example. Imagine you were having an EEG run while listening to beautiful harp music. Suddenly the music changes to a loud, heavy metal group. Can you see how the EEG might change as the body responds to the music? The body is very sensitive to vibrational changes. This is why Homeopathy works so well.

X-Ray- Electromagnetic energy in the X-ray frequency is projected through a body part to be analyzed and the rays are collected on a film or photographic plate. Various body tissues absorb the radiation at different rates, causing various shadows to appear on the film. The greater the density of the tissue, the more radiopaque (whiter or lighter) the area appears on the film. An example would be: the enamel of a tooth appears more radiopaque (whiter) than the alveolar bone supporting the tooth. When decay is detected in a radiograph, it is seen as a radiolucent (dark shadow) area on the radiopaque (white) enamel. The density of metal is so great that the area is displayed on the film as a radiopaque area at its maximum.

Acupuncture point identification- Acupuncture points can be found by introducing a low voltage electrical charge into the body and then measuring the electrical conductance of the skin. The acupuncture points are more conductive (there is less electrical resistance) than the surrounding tissue. This was proven by Dr. W.A. Tiller, past president of the Material Science department at Stanford University.

The Chinese identified unique energy pathways that connect the hands and feet to major organ systems. These pathways are called meridians. The Chinese said the meridians were channels of energy or **Chi**. Each meridian was a window to the status of an organ or system in the body.

EAV (Electroacupuncture According to Voll) testing- In the early 1950's, Reinhold Voll, a German medical doctor and dentist became interested in acupuncture. He developed the technology of using an ohm meter for finding acupuncture points electrically. He was extremely successful in finding acupuncture points with his machine. He demonstrated that these points, known to Chinese acupuncturists, had a different resistance to a tiny electrical current passed through the body than the adjacent tissues.[1] Voll discovered and proved that electrical changes in certain acupuncture points could be associated with certain diseases. Then he was able to identify those diseases earlier when treatment was likely to be more effective. Voll published a great deal of information about using the acupuncture points diagnostically. (Until Voll, these points had been used mainly for treatment.) He found certain points showed abnormal readings when subjects were reacting to substances. He made several discoveries related to "allergy" testing. Not all of Voll's points are acupuncture points. He identified over 1,000 points and these points are called Voll points.

Kim Bong Han proved the meridians existed by injecting a radioisotope into an acupuncture point and imaging a system of ducts that did not follow an artery, vein or even a nerve path. The flow was, in fact, mapped out thousands of years ago and was following an energetic path called a meridian. Han proved the meridian system connects with all cell nuclei in the body.

Dr. Robert Boecker authored "The Body Electric". He studied currents in the body and found that they changed after an injury. He found the meridians flowing through the mesenchyme. Taber's defines the mesenchyme as *a diffuse network of cells giving rise to the connective tissues, blood and blood vessels, and the lymphatic system.*

In 1984, researchers from the University of Hawaii compared six different diagnostic modalities for assessing food allergies. These tests included patient health history, food challenge, skin, RAST, IgE antibodies and electrodermal testing. The testing was done in a double blind fashion with the patients not knowing what antigens were being tested and the instrument operator not knowing anything about the patient's food sensitivities. In over 300 tests, electrodermal testing matched the patient health history 74% of the time, the food rechallenge test 77% of the time, skin testing 71% of the time and the RAST testing 69% of the time. The authors concluded that, "The EAV (electrodermal testing) data obtained in this experiment demonstrates the highest degree of compatibility with the food challenge test, which is considered to be the most sensitive of the currently available diagnostic techniques for food allergy." In addition, the EAV tests were comparable with both the skin and RAST tests.[2]

Dr. William Tiller, Past President of the Material Science Department of Stanford University set out to disprove Voll's work. His research found inflammation of an organ caused an increase of ions which enhanced electrical flow of electrons and was measured as an elevated reading on Voll's equipment. Degeneration of an organ caused decreased ion concentrations that seem to hinder the flow of electrons and reduce the conductivity; this produced low readings on Voll's equipment. Dr. Tiller became an advocate of the technology Voll developed.

Dr. Voll with his wealth of dental and medical knowledge, discovered that every tooth in the mouth relates to a specific meridian. Infected or diseased teeth could alter the health of other organs located on that meridian. He also held that an organ with dysfunction could alter the health of a tooth on that meridian. Here we will refer to a chart found on the next page, mapping the correlation of each of the teeth with the specific organs on that meridian.[3]

You will notice the meridian crosses from the mandibular molars to the maxillary bicuspids and from the maxillary molars to the mandibular bicuspids. This is because the Large Intestine meridian goes from the corner of the nares down the arm to the finger. The Stomach meridian starts under the eye and goes straight down the face past the nipple to the toe.

Tooth Meridian Chart

RIGHT SIDE — LEFT SIDE

Tooth 1: Heart, Small Intest., Duodenum, Shoulder, Elbow

Teeth 2, 3: Pancreas, Stomach, Oropharynx, Max. Sinus, Larynx

Teeth 4, 5: Lung, Large Intest, Nose, Ethmoid Sinus, Bronchi

Tooth 6: Liver, Gallbladder, Eye, Hip, Knee, Sphen. Sinus

Teeth 7, 8: Kidney, Bladder, Urogenital, FrontalSinus

Teeth 9, 10: Kidney, Bladder, Urogenital, Frontal Sinus

Tooth 11: Liver, Gallbladder, Eye, Hip, Knee, Spen. Sinus

Teeth 12, 13: Lung, Large Intest., Nose, Ethmoid Sinus, Bronchi

Teeth 14, 15: Spleen, Stomach, Oropharynx, Max. Sinus, Larynx

Tooth 16: Heart, Small Intest., Jejunum, Ileum, Shoulder, Elbow

Tooth 17: Heart, Small Intest., Jejunum, Ileum, Shoulder, Elbow

Teeth 18, 19: Lung, Large Intest., Nose, Ethmoid Sinus, Bronchi

Teeth 20, 21: Spleen, Stomach, Oropharynx, Max. Sinus, Larynx

Tooth 22: Liver, Gallbladder, Eye, Hip, Knee, Sphen. Sinuse

Teeth 23, 24: Kidney, Bladder, Urogenital, Frontal Sinus

Teeth 25, 26: Kidney, Bladder, Urogenital, Frontal Sinus

Tooth 27: Liver, Gallbladder, Eye, Hip, Knee, Sphen. Sinus

Teeth 28, 29: Pancreas, Stomach, Oropharynx, Max. Sinus, Larynx

Teeth 30, 31: Lung, Large Intest., Nose, Ethmoid Sinus, Bronchi

Tooth 32: Heart, Small Intest., Duodenum, Shoulder, Elbow

WHAT DENTAL CONDITIONS EFFECT

BIOENERGETICS?

ABSCESSES, INFECTIONS OF TEETH AND FISTULAS

TOOTH DECAY

ROOT CANALS

CAVITATIONS

HEAVY METALS

GALVANISM

ORTHODONTICS

IMPLANTS

DENTURES

TRAUMA

TMJ

FIXED BRIDGES

ALLERGIES

CHAPTER THREE

INFECTIONS OF TEETH

CAUSES OF TOOTH DEATH

Teeth can be traumatized in different ways. A direct blow of force or decay, are the primary causes leading to the death of a nerve in a tooth. There are several other reasons that a tooth may die.

Some death can be attributed to iatrogenic causes. **1)** The tooth can be heated too much during the drilling process. Some teeth can not recover and may slowly die over the course of several years. **2)** The use of high speed drilling may cause a vacuum effect and suck healthy tissue out of the tubules of the teeth. This allows those empty tubules to fill with impurities and destroy the tooth. Dr. Doug Cook DDS is a Biological dentist promoting the use of slow speed drilling. **3)** Placement of a crown on a tooth may smother the tooth. Fluid actually moves from the center of the tooth to the outside, in a sense detoxing. In a sick tooth you will see the movement of fluid from outside toward the center, bringing in bacteria. Placing a crown on a tooth compromises the tooth's ability to detoxify or breathe.

Death of a tooth can also be caused by an organ that shares the same meridian, if that organ is ill. This can cause a blockage of energy. The blockage can prevent energy reaching the tooth associated with that meridian. This blockage of energy will finally kill the tooth. An example would be a smoker with chronic lung disease. It is very possible for the teeth on the lung meridian to die. They might not even have dental restorations in them. When a perfectly good, unrestored tooth abscesses, look at the organs on that meridian.

Poor occlusion due to a bad bite or the poor match of the chewing surfaces of the teeth can cause death of teeth. The constant trauma of the teeth hitting improperly causes bruising. Over years this trauma may be the cause of tooth death.

The spread of an osteonecrotic lesion (dead or diseased

31

bone) under a vital tooth can cause a tooth to die. The bacteria from these lesions can spread through good bone, leaving areas of gangrenous (dead) tissue around a healthy tooth. This ultimately kills off the blood supply to the healthy tooth and it dies.

What Happens When A Tooth Dies?

Regardless of the cause of death, a long standing, chronic degeneration may cause the patient little to no symptoms of an ongoing infection. The patient may not have any pain. As the nerve dies, toxins are released from the necrotic tissue. In a **chronic state** the process may cause slow bone destruction, allowing a *void* or _holding_ *area*, filled with festered material to be formed. Toxins are picked up and carried throughout the body via the blood stream that passes by the dump site, 24 hours a day 7 days a week. An example of a slow death could be, a front tooth injured in a car accident. As the years go by, the tooth may appear darker. X-ray may show a calcified, dead pulp chamber in the tooth or may even show a void of bone at the tip of the root, filled with gangrenous tissue. This tooth is now termed "Abscessed." Upon removal of the tooth, it is common to find a radicular cyst. This was the body's attempt to contain the purulent material in a sack - a valiant effort towards self preservation. This process was so slow that the body adjusted to the condition. It is not uncommon for these teeth to be pain free.

In an **acute situation**, no *void* or *holding area* exists large enough to accommodate the large quantity of purulent matter. Creating pressure beneath gum and bone, the body creates an opening or drainage port to vent, called a **fistula**. Fistulas seen in the mouth, are channels that carry pus from the infected area to the outside of the face or mouth. Giving the appearance of a boil or a pimple, this vent allows the body to drain away excessive amounts of pus. This tooth is now termed "Abscessed." This *is very similar to a volcanic eruption with lava finding a path to escape.* If a fistula does not present, then you may see extreme swelling in the infected area.

In either case (chronic or acute) the ensuing infection causes disturbances on the entire meridian. The energy traveling on the meridian now sees the infected area and tries to get through. Like a traffic jam, some of the energy will slowly get through and some will try to detour. Those that detour, go around the blockage, back to the meridian on the other side of the infection. This slowing of energy or detouring causes stress on the body. Our body can handle some stress but it does have a limit.

By means of x-rays and clinical examination, it is extremely difficult to ascertain changes in the dentin and pulp when severe morphological signs are not observable. The dentist uses the x-ray to look for widening of the periodontal ligament surrounding the tooth, narrowing of the canals, granulomas, cysts and condensing osteitis. Since energetic processes always precede the detectable morphological changes, an EAV test could be of great assistance giving a picture of the status in the pulp and dentin.

It has been my experience of 26 years in dentistry, that conventional dentistry does not have the means to accurately determine the vitality of a tooth. There are many occasions when people are capable of detecting a cavity in their own mouth before it shows on x-ray. It is these sensitive people that also come to the dentist with the complaint of a toothache and a sense of impending doom. After being subjected to multiple x-rays, percussion tests, and temperature tests, if nothing is conclusive, the dentist is either going to refer the person to an endodontic specialist for further evaluation or send them home.

It was with horror that I recently met a woman who had 4 root canal teeth in a row. She could not precisely pinpoint the location of pain but insisted the dentist do something. In vain, the dentist performed a root canal on the tooth she thought was bothering her. She returned the next week to have a second tooth treated, then a third and finally a fourth root canal. On the fourth try her pain abated. Wouldn't it be in the interest of health to pursue the validity of the claims made by EAV testing?[4] I personally have witnessed patients referred to a dental practice by doctors that make use of EAV; told to seek their expertise in the removal of a tooth that by all standard testing shows vital. Upon removal, the tooth was sectioned to find necrotic pulp or calcified canals, proving the accuracy of the diagnosis from the referring doctor.

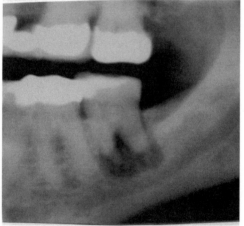

This x-ray shows an infection of a molar, note the dark area below the last tooth.

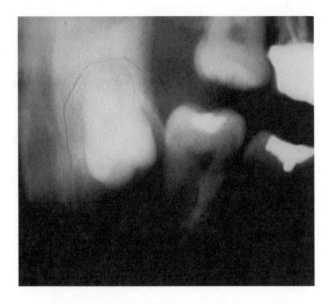

Inverted wisdom tooth that is impacted with a cyst

CHAPTER FOUR

ROOT CANALS

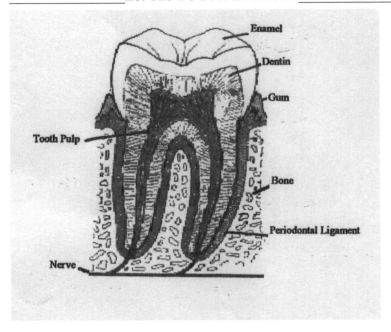

Enamel

Dentin

Gum

Tooth Pulp

Bone

Periodontal Ligament

Nerve

DIAGRAM OF A HEALTHY TOOTH

Teeth are living tissues covered with a layer of enamel above the gum line for strength and protection of the delicate tissues within.

How is a Root Canal Done?

The traditional dentist goes to great extremes to save a tooth, even if it means embalming it to preserve a lifeless skeleton. A small hole is drilled into the center of the tooth through the top or chewing surface. This allows limited access to the inner chamber of the tooth that contains the nerve, lymph and blood vessels. From this chamber a pathway, called a **canal**, runs to the tip of the root, which is the entry point for the vessels. Typically, anterior (the front six) teeth have a single canal and posterior (back) teeth have two to four canals, depending on the tooth and its location. An attempt to remove the necrotic or gangrenous tissue is made by the use of a small file to clean the main canals. A problem overlooked in the past is that the inside of the tooth contains miles of tiny tubules. The tubules run perpendicular to the canals and can not be cleaned. The diameter of the tubules is large enough for 12-13 bacteria to fit side by side but too small for even one white blood cell. Antibiotics are of no use because the blood supply in the tooth was removed. How would you get the antibiotic to the area without a blood supply? Conventional dentistry tries to ignore this fact by sealing the tooth, creating a tomb. This tomb is filled with anaerobic bacteria (This is bacteria that live without oxygen) capable of multiplying and finding a vent to escape. This vent could be a micro fracture in the wall of the tooth or an ineffective seal in a canal that can allow bacteria to escape through the apex (the tip of the root).

Thioether and Mercaptan are gases given off by root canal teeth. These gases were used in the World Wars as neurotoxins. This may seem a small stress. You will see how those stresses add up.

For many years the most common material used to seal the canal was gutta percha; it is still widely used. Gutta percha is a rubbery- like substance that is easily packed into the tooth when the material is somewhat warmed. However, when it cools and sets for a few days, shrinkage occurs, allowing bacteria to escape, through the apex of the tooth. This means a chronic low grade infection or toxic material may be picked up by blood cells as they are passing by the area and distributed throughout the entire body. These bacteria, now mobile via the blood, are capable of causing a secondary infection in the body by infecting the heart, kidneys, joints, nervous system, brain, eyes and may endanger pregnant women.

Some Biological dentists are using a newer material called Biocalix. This material was believed to kill the bacteria in the tubules. Research now shows it only buys a year to a year and a half of time and then the bacteria begins to breed at a rapid rate.

There are dentists using lasers to reduce bacteria, they promise the procedure will kill the bacteria in the root canals before filling them. Some of these dentists even make claims that they sterilize the tooth by using the laser. This has now proven a **failure** for **long term permanent** solutions. We removed a tooth less than 2 months after it was treated by laser and deemed sterile. The results from Affinity Labeling Technologies showed the tooth was still severely toxic. Check www.dentalhelp.org for more information. Biocalix and laser treatment of root canals seemed promising at one time, but that is no longer the case.

Even if you could sterilize the canals and solve the bacterial part of the problem of the root canal, it does not eliminate the problem of the energy blockage. Electricity does not flow through dead tissue!

Think of an 18 wheeler stuck sideways on a major freeway. The root canal tooth leaking bacteria would be like the stalled truck carrying a hazardous material. The mythical sterile root canal tooth is an empty stalled truck. Not as hazardous but nonetheless it is blocking the flow of traffic.

All of the teeth are on the meridian pathways. A dead tooth can cause a blockage on the meridian. This blockage prevents the free flow of energy to all the organs on that meridian.[5] As a result of an infection in a maxillary first molar, energy may be blocked to the stomach or breast, as they are on the same meridian pathway. Recent studies involving 60 women with breast cancer showed 57 of these women had a root canal on a tooth related to the breast meridian.

A good percentage of root canals are performed with little to no immediate problem for the patient. Even if the tooth is sealed tight, preventing the escape of bacteria and toxins, the energy can't get through the dead mass to conduct impulses to the rest of the organs on that meridian.

This lack of conduction of electrical impulses through dead tissue is best illustrated in the heart. Seeing those areas of non-conductance on an EKG, enables the cardiologist to precisely pinpoint and diagnose the area of damage to the heart. Is he actually looking at the heart? No, he is looking at the flow of electricity through the heart.

Imagine an arm with the blood supply and nerves removed. Would you keep a non-vital, stuffed, dead limb? I can not think of another medical procedure that hollows out an organ, stuffs it and leaves it in your body. I know that I seem a bit dramatic here. It is very demanding on your body to try to compensate for this blockage of energy on that meridian. As if this stress of energy being blocked was not enough, add poor diet, lack of exercise or rest. Well now, add exposure to chemicals in our water, food and air and you might understand why some immune systems finally max out.

Can A Root Canal Fail?

There are a percentage of root canals that fail or re-abscess. When this happens the bacteria finds a vent to escape (usually through the tip of the root) and these toxins can cause bone destruction. Remember, this is usually pain-free because the nerve was removed! Ignoring the problem may lead to such massive bone destruction to the maxilla or mandible that the tooth will become loose, due to lack of bony support. In the case of re-infection the prognosis is not good unless a procedure called an apicoectomy is done. In addition, if a large area of bone is destroyed, a bone augmentation may be done. An apicoectomy is a surgical treatment. This involves making an incision in the gum near the tip of the root and debriding the infected area. Usually the tip of the root is removed and the tooth is retro-filled. Retro-filling means, a filling is placed into the tip of the root, essentially filling it from the bottom, up. The material used to fill this by conventional dentists is Silver Amalgam. Yes, a mercury filling, placed directly into the bone itself! This is a heroic attempt to seal the bacteria inside the tooth. Again, if the tooth has a micro fracture vent available (like a crack in the tooth), then the surgery is destined to fail. Unfortunately, these micro fractures are undetectable in the majority of cases until the inevitable removal of the tooth is done and the fracture is found.

It seems that an extraction is a suitable option instead of the root canal being performed in the first place. One must consider the patient's philosophy on health. Do they want to outlive their teeth or have the teeth outlive them? Cost is a consideration to most people, so I will allow it to enter into the picture. A root canal may run between $250 - $800 depending on the number of canals the tooth has. Front teeth usually have one canal; bicuspids can have two canals, and the molars can have as many as five canals. Now, because the tooth no longer has a blood supply, it will become brittle. In order to prevent the tooth from breaking off at the gum line, a crown is placed on top of the tooth for added strength, at a cost of $550 - $1,000. If the root canal fails, the apicoectomy can run as high as $1,200. This may not be the end. If all of this fails, there will be the fee for an extraction of $250 - $1,200.

Removal of a root canal tooth can be very difficult. As I stated before, the tooth becomes very brittle due to the removal of the blood supply. The root canal teeth often break in pieces during the extraction adding to the trauma for the patient and the body. Removal of the tooth, prior to the root canal, would be much kinder to the body, and placement of a removable appliance would be a cost effective alternative to the entire experience.

Are there times that I suggest a root canal would be in the patient's best interest? Yes; again we must consider the patient as a whole. A young woman engaged to be married in two weeks, breaks two front teeth in a car accident. She is otherwise healthy with no major immune system complications. The trauma of having the teeth extracted so close to her wedding, may be more of an immediate burden to her immune system than a root canal. At least for a while. She could be informed of the possibility of future extraction which would mentally give her time to handle the trauma. Certainly she should be informed that the area involves a meridian related to, in this case, kidney, bladder, and uterus. If she starts having health complications in those areas the burden of keeping those root canal teeth should be reconsidered.

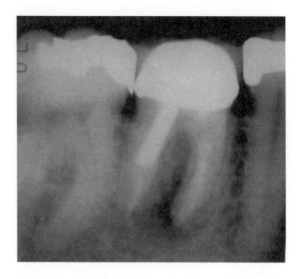

Root Canal on a Lower Molar with infection still apparent

CHAPTER FIVE

CAVITATIONS

WHAT IS A CAVITATION?

Bone is connected to bone by a ligament. Teeth, being calcium structures, are linked to the jaw bones by means of ligaments called periodontal ligaments.

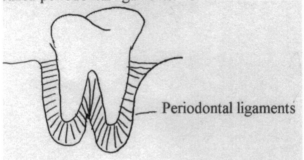

— Periodontal ligaments

When a tooth is extracted and the periodontal ligament, along with any unhealthy bone is removed, a message is sent to the cells in that area to increase osteoblasts (cells that build bone) for new bone to be regenerated. If the periodontal ligament or unhealthy bone is not removed, the signal to the body to generate new bone is interrupted and new bone formation is hampered.

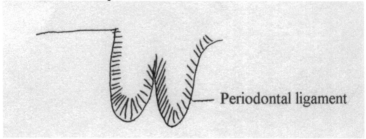

— Periodontal ligament

As time passes, new bone may fill in a few millimeters on the very top of the hole (but not near the old ligament) and form a thin layer of cortical bone. New gum tissue will grow over the top of the cortical bone leaving a hidden cavern underneath called a "Cavitation".

This may lead to a low grade, chronic, inflammatory process. The flow of energy is again an issue. This area is osteonecrotic (dead bone with no blood supply). Remember, energy does not go through dead tissue. The area will require surgical treatment to clear the debris and the blockage of energy.

Have you ever purchased a battery operated watch that has a small piece of plastic between the battery and the watch terminal? The plastic prevents the energy in the battery from making contact with the watch terminal. No contact means no message sent to the rest of the watch to make it work, so the watch sits idle. All the pieces are there and all that needs to be done is to remove the plastic. Once the plastic is removed and contact made, the energy flows into the watch and it works. In this case, the plastic was the dead tissue or energy block.

This periodontal ligament (like the plastic), is the barrier preventing contact from the bone on the one side of the ligament to the extraction site on the other side of the ligament. The blood vessels can't get through the periodontal ligament to carry away the blood clot in the socket. This means the material is not dissolved and carried away by the body; instead, it rots. No antibiotic will help because the antibiotic in the blood can not get past the ligament to reach the site. This becomes "Osteonecrosis". This term is used for areas of bone that lack a blood supply. Osteo is Latin for bone. Necrotic tissue is dead tissue. Evidence now confirms many of these areas to be Osteomyelitis. Osteomyelitis is a bacterial infection of the bone.

Osteonecrosis is different from osteoporosis. Whereas osteonecrosis is a hole in the bone, osteoporosis is a thinning of the bone cells throughout the bone. Visualize a piece of thick, white linen material. This represents healthy bone. Now visualize a piece of sheer nylon like women's pantyhose. This represents osteoporosis. A hole or runner in either material would be osteonecrosis, a void of the desired material.

Other things can effect the extraction site from filling in with healthy bone. 1) Clotting problems due to a deficiency of proteins. Proteins are essential for growth, the building of new tissue and the repair of injured or broken down tissue. 2) Hypofibrinolysis- poor dissolving of the blood clot by proteolytic enzymes. 3) Introduction of bacteria into the surgical site. Remember those water filters. 4) Morphing; or the changing of aerobic bacteria to anaerobic.

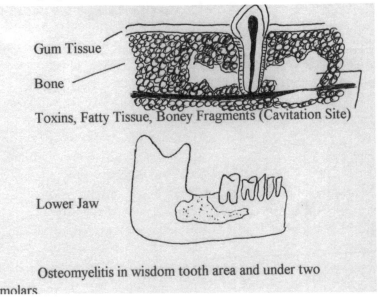

Gum Tissue

Bone

Toxins, Fatty Tissue, Boney Fragments (Cavitation Site)

Lower Jaw

Osteomyelitis in wisdom tooth area and under two molars

DIAGNOSIS

Diagnosis is not always possible with the exclusive use of x-rays. In order for a cavitation to show on x-ray there must be at least a 30% loss of bone. This area may fill with toxic tissue and/or heavy metals, giving the appearance of a greater density than actually exists. When it is visible on x-ray, it usually presents as a poorly defined area. It is very difficult if not impossible to diagnose cavitations with x-ray.

This is where Applied Kinesiology (Muscle Testing) or Electro Acupuncture According to Voll (EAV) can act as tools to help determine the burden.

There is another technology called CAVITAT. Bob Jones developed a machine that can take digital imaging of the diseased alveolar jawbone. It is a noninvasive technique using speed of sound frequency to document the varying degrees of necrosis in the jaw with a photo image. The sound waves are sent through the bone via a very small transducer which is pressed against the cheek. Inside the mouth rests a digitalized array, capable of interpreting the strength of the signal after it has passed through the bone. Once this signal is captured, it is sent to the computer which converts it to a three-dimensional colored image. It is capable of detecting jawbone defects down to 1/32nd of an inch in diameter. Other methods used for detecting lesions in the jaws are CAT scans and MRI's which use radiation and provide only a one-dimensional perspective.

Tests on over 7,000 sites reveal information proving every root canal tooth has osteonecrosis around the root tip. The investigations done to satisfy the FDA showed 94% of old extraction sites were positive for bone lesions. These areas were confirmed by postsurgical biopsy reports. The FDA was so moved by the research presented that it mandated treatment of Level 3 and Level 4 lesions found by CAVITAT be a surgical intervention. Now mind you; that makes this a disease of epidemic proportions that the American Dental Association does not teach or recognize.

The latest scientific research has proven these lesions are highly neurotoxic. These toxins inhibit protein and enzyme absorption essential for cellular functions that may contribute to or induce systemic diseases. Remember, this necrotic area can spread!

Bob's invention is a direct result of his own experience with cavitations. Bob was diagnosed with probable ALS (Lou Gehrig's disease). He was in a wheelchair, unable to walk more than 20 feet without collapsing. Bob had his amalgams and his root canal teeth removed. His cavitations were cleaned out and he had chelation therapy. Today, Bob is walking and working, eager to share his story. He travels and speaks internationally to physicians and dentists, spreading word of his technology. His mission is one of health for all. Bob came to Houston when the local ABC affiliate was televising "The Debra Duncan Show". They featured this book and the health problems dentistry can cause. The show was titled "Let The Tooth Be Known". Bob was a guest on that show and it was their most requested rerun. For more information on CAVITAT go to www.cavitat.com

DIAGNOSTIC BLOCKS

Sometimes a local anesthetic is injected in the area of the cavitation to confirm the electrical blockage. Picture a car; it just won't start. Is it the engine or the ignition switch? If we bypass the ignition switch, hot wire the car and it runs, then we know it was the ignition switch. This is what happens with a cavitation or a root canal. Energy can not go on the normal path so it must slow or detour, expending energy and creating stress for the body. The injection of anesthesia provides a short circuit, taking the blockage out of the picture for a smooth flow of energy. Another advantage of using the anesthesia is that it increases the cellular membrane permeability. This increased permeability allows the energy to flow with ease, even in areas that are blocked, by increasing the conductivity. This is a great diagnostic tool when constant pain is an issue. Pain reduction after placement of the anesthetic around the suspected cavitation site is seen as a positive result. An example would be severe pain in a shoulder dissipating after injecting the upper third molar area, in as much as they are on the same meridian. The absence of pain in the shoulder after the injection would help confirm an interference field at the injected site. Many results are quite dramatic as the stress of trying to send energy past the blockage is removed.

HOW DO YOU TREAT CAVITATIONS?

There are four classifications or grade levels of cavitations. Grade one has light ischemia or diminished circulation and grade four has frank dead bone. There seems to be hope for grade one and two lesions by increasing blood flow to the jaw. This has been documented by taking CAVITAT images, then using an anodyne (monochromatic laser) and reimaging with the CAVITAT. This type of laser increases circulation and may prove beneficial in healing an area. As this book is being written, I am designing a study using proteolytic enzymes to act as thinners and increase circulation to the jaw. Again, the CAVITAT will be one of the monitoring devices.

To treat a grade three or four cavitation, the dentist makes an incision through the gum with a scalpel and then uses a small instrument to go through the overlay of bone. If the area had filled in with healthy bone, the area would be a dense matrix of bone. Removing the overlay will expose the osteonecrotic lesion. Sometimes, the regeneration of bone has been so hampered and incomplete that the cavitation site, no matter how old, still has the appearance of the tooth having just been removed with holes for each of the roots.

The term NICO is used by many dentists when talking about cavitations. NICO "neuralgia inducing cavitational osteonecrosis" really refers to the neuralgia symptoms that many of these lesions cause. This is the term used only when these bone lesions cause facial pain.

The clinical and histopathological features of NICO more closely resemble ischemic, avascular, aseptic osteonecrosis. This is because there is no blood supply to that area of the bone. Tabor's medical dictionary defines *ischemic* - anemia due to obstruction of the circulation of a part. The term *avascular* - lacking in blood supply or having a poor blood supply. The more appropriate term for these areas, commonly called NICO, is Osteonecrosis. *Osteonecrosis* is defined as death of bone tissue in mass. A term more familiar to people is gangrenous. Gangrene is defined as the death of tissue usually due to deficient or absent blood supply. The similarity to ischemic osteonecrosis is so strong as to lend considerable credence to the theory that NICOs result from poor vascular circulation.

Some individuals have genetic clotting disorders that create small micro-clots of blood in the jaw. These blood clots lodge in the jaw and cause death to the surrounding bone. These same blood clots could lodge in a heart or brain making these patients at higher risk for heart attack or stroke.

Another term for these lesions is Bone Marrow Edema. In Bone Marrow Edema the problem is due to poor outflow of blood in the area. A similar type problem happens with asthma;

where instead of poor outflow of blood, it is air. The air gets into the alveoli in the lungs as the asthmatic takes a breath. The problem is getting the air back out, thus the asthma patient wheezes as the person tries to exhale. When this happens in the jaw it causes tissue death to the surrounding bone.

Sometimes the cavitation site is filled with necrotic tissue or an oily substance. Occasionally fat can be seen floating to the surface of the opening. The bone has a gritty, sawdust- like consistency. The bone may feel like styrofoam or like a mush. The area may contain some small chips of dead bone, bacteria and other matter.

The dentist must remove the old ligament and unhealthy bone thus cleaning the site. This may be difficult to do as the dentist must go by feel. Often times a small tunnel or worm hole will be found coming from the site. This must be followed and cleaned out. The dentist is working in a deep hole and it is often difficult to visualize or determine when he is through removing all the debris. Use of Applied Kinesiology (Muscle Testing) or Electro Dermal Screening (EDS) is of enormous value. After surgical debriding, the site is now ready for the body to take over the healing process.[6] Now, antibiotics can get to the area, and in some cases, they may be required. The use of homeopathic drainage remedies and autosodes work very well in assisting the healing process.

To avoid forming a cavitation, complete removal of the periodontal ligament and curettage of the bone is recommended after every extraction. This complete cleanout is especially important if there is a chronic bone problem near endodontic teeth or periodontally involved teeth.

To date there is no documentation of bone regeneration in level three or four lesions by any means other than surgery.

For more information about NICO or Osteonecrotic lesions see www.maxillofacialcenter.com/NICOhome.html

CHAPTER SIX

HEAVY METALS

MERCURY

The modern silver amalgam filling (amalgam, meaning a mixture of several different metals with mercury), traditionally known as a silver filling, has been used as the primary restorative material for over 180 years and accounts for about 75% of all tooth restorations. Amalgam fillings contain about 50% mercury by weight, 35% silver, 13% tin, 2% copper and a trace of zinc.[7] Researchers from all over the world have measured mercury vapor coming off the dental fillings, particularly after chewing, brushing or after eating hot or acidic foods. This can be measured with a piece of equipment called a vapor sniffer. The patient will have a reading taken before chewing. A second reading is taken after chewing to show the level of mercury vapor. Everyone knows that mercury is a poison. **Mercury is extremely toxic**. Sharma and Obersteiner at Utah State University discovered mercury as the single most toxic metal that they investigated.[8]

A single amalgam filling weighs about 1 Gram and contains 1/2 Gram of Mercury. The average adult has 10 fillings. When we are looking at the toxic load; let me put it so you can understand. If 1/2 Gram of Mercury were found in a 10 acre lake it would warrant a fish advisory. In 1994 the Minnesota legislature placed a ban on running shoes with Mercury lights because they contained 1/2 Gram of Mercury

The world's foremost researchers on mercury toxicity, Drs. Thomas Clarkson and John Hursh of the University of Rochester School of Medicine, Department of Toxicology and Drs. Magnus Nylander and Lars Friberg of Karolinska Institute in Stockholm, Sweden, concluded from their research that "the release of mercury from dental amalgams makes the predominant contribution to human exposure to inorganic mercury including mercury vapor in the general population." Autopsy studies show a correlation between the number of

54

silver dental fillings and the mercury levels in the brain.[9] [10] Ever hear of the phrase "Mad Hatter"? Hat makers used to use mercury and had direct exposure with their hands. High levels were in the brain tissue and thus the saying, "Mad as a hatter", meaning they were crazy. Mercury lowers the levels of Serotonin, (a neurotransmitter in the brain). Low levels of Serotonin are implicated with violent behavior, depression, alcoholism, and other disorders. An ongoing research project at the University of Kentucky suggests that mercury may be a contributing factor in people getting Alzheimer's, as they have higher levels of mercury in their brains.[11] The Second Nordic Symposium on Trace Elements in Human Health and Disease from August of 1987 in Odense, Denmark showed that Multiple Sclerosis patients have been shown to have 8 times higher levels of mercury in the cerebrospinal fluid compared to neurologically healthy control subjects. For more information about MS and Dental check out the following website-www.altcorp.com/slideshows/toxins/sld006.htm

A major study conducted jointly by the University of Calgary and two U.S. universities, Georgia and Tufts, recently reported that the mercury placed in monkey's teeth triggered the test animals' resistance to antibiotics. Antibiotic resistance is a growing problem in medicine today. Mercury can bind to the DNA (deoxyribonucleic acid) of cells as well as to the membranes causing disfigurement and interfering with normal cell function. When this happens, the immune system no longer recognizes the cell as part of the body and will attack it.[12]

In America, during the 1800's, concern about mercury toxicity caused the American Society of Dental Surgeons to make mercury usage an issue of malpractice, mandating that its members sign an oath not to use mercury-containing materials.[13] Yes, read that again, the 1800's! Even with all of this, use of mercury fillings increased because this cheaper material offered dentists that did use it an economic advantage and it was very durable in the mouth. It changed dentistry from an industry that only served the well to do with gold fillings, to a profession that could serve the populace at large. By 1856, the American Society of Dental Surgeons was forced to disband due to dwindling membership over the mercury filling issue. In its place, arose the American Dental Association, founded by those that advocated mercury use in dentistry.[14] [15] Was their motive to better serve the poor? Did you know the ADA holds a patent on amalgam filling material?

Other countries seem to be ahead of the United States when it comes to banning mercury in dentistry. In 1987 the Swedish government announced that steps would be taken to eliminate amalgam usage and banned its use all together in 1989. If you are a citizen of Sweden, the government pays 50% of the cost for the removal of amalgams. Finding it cheaper than paying for the long term health maladies that the mercury toxicity causes.[16] In January 1992, the Germans announced their intention to ban amalgams.[17] The Austrian Minister of Health announced a deadline for banning amalgam usage.[18] In 1995, Health Canada (a federal agency) assessed amalgam risks and recommended limiting the number of amalgams according to age. They felt the tolerable daily intake of mercury vapor is four fillings for an adult and less for children.[19] Studies by the World Health Organization show that a single amalgam can release three to seventeen micrograms of mercury per day, making dental amalgam a major source of mercury exposure.

So what is the standing of the United States? The American Dental Association's stand is: Exposure to mercury from amalgams is harmless. The ADA pleaded in a Court of Law that it has no legal duty to protect the public from allegedly dangerous materials used in dentistry. When the

ADA was confronted with the fact that the maximum exposure to mercury vapors is exceeded by patients with mercury silver fillings in their mouths, the ADA petitioned the Agency for Toxic Substances and Disease Registry (ATSDR) to raise the Minimum Risk Level (MRL) by almost 15 fold. The Federal Drug Administration must go by the information on the Material Safety Data Sheets provided by the manufacturer of the materials. Dentsply/ Caulk manufactures amalgam filling material for sale to dentists.

The MSDS information is available on the internet, @ www.caulk.com/MSDSDFU/DispersalloyMSDS.html#MERC. The manufacturers of amalgams suggest not using amalgam in the mouth next to a tooth with any gold or other metal (because of the galvanic reaction, which moves mercury out of the filling faster). The manufacturers do not want it used in children under six years of age or in pregnant women. They even go so far as to say that removal of amalgams should be avoided in the pregnant patient. They recommend the number of amalgam fillings for any one patient be kept to a minimum. So the information given to the FDA by the manufacturer is in conflict with the information that the ADA is giving. The FDA must follow the manufacturer.

Amalgam fillings contain five toxic metals- Copper, Tin, Silver, Zinc and Mercury. We will discuss these other metals in the next portion so keep reading.

Why aren't all dentists willing to change to safer materials on their own? Some dentists are unwilling to believe that our government would allow amalgam use if it were unsafe. Because they believe this, these dentists are very sincere when assuring patients it is safe. I wonder what they would say if they had all the facts? Let's look at the German dentists. As the government voted on the ban of mercury, the dentists lobbied. They wanted to retain use of mercury fillings.

The wise lawmakers weighed the evidence against mercury and rewrote the law. If the dentist places a material in the mouth and the patient can prove his health suffered from that material, the dentist would be held personally responsible. With the law written this way, you will not find a dentist willing to take the risk of placing the mercury fillings. Just like most people, the dentists do not like to admit that they are wrong. Especially when," It has been done that way for more than 150 years." Learning to use new materials involves some retraining on the dentists' part. It means taking off work to attend continuing education seminars. The alternative to amalgam use is not cost effective for the dentist, because insurance won't pay for the more expensive materials. Could part of the reason that the US is behind be that they are afraid of the legal implications? *Look what happened with Silicone implants.*

There is hope. New Hampshire's Governor signed a law that was enacted January 1, 2002 "No dentist may place an amalgam larger than one Gram and if it is under one Gram they must inform the patient of the possible hazards". In the summer of 2000, a Maryland judge ruled that the Maryland State Board of Dental examiners violated the law by prohibiting dentists from discussing the risks of amalgam fillings. Arizona passed Senate Bill 1155 into law- This mandates an Arizona dentist that places an amalgam must inform the patient that the filling is about 50% mercury and that mercury is acknowledged to travel to body tissues causing undetermined health problems. Maine's new law requires dentists to distribute informational brochures about the dangers of mercury fillings. In 1986 California passed Proposition 65 which was amended to include amalgam fillings in 1996. This required dentists to post warning signs in waiting rooms. The signs were never posted because the California Dental Board never followed through with creating the literature. In June of 2001 the California

Legislature voted to dismiss the members serving on the board and replace them for their failure to adopt and create the fact sheet. California's Governor Davis signed the law and was quoted "Mercury is a persistent and toxic pollutant that bioaccumulates in the environment...".

The Environmental Protection Agency says that amalgam removed from a patient has so much mercury that it is a waste disposal hazard. This means you can't throw it in the trash, bury it in the ground, pour it down the drain or put it in a landfill. How is it possible that it can be safe to be in your mouth? It is a hazardous material before it goes in your mouth - *safe as it is in your mouth* and hazardous as it is removed? What do you think? The Occupational Safety and Health Administration requires very specific guidelines to be followed for the dental employee working around removal of old amalgams or placement of new ones. 1) **Salvage of all scrap amalgam must be stored in an airtight container with water covering the amalgam.** *(This prevents release of mercury vapors)* 2) **Use of a no touch technique.** *This requires use of gloves while handling amalgam.* 3) **A well-ventilated work area** 4) **Alert all personnel involved in the handling of amalgam of the potential hazard of mercury vapors.** 5) **Have periodic mercury vapor level tests made in operatories.** *(Vapor levels are recommended, not mandatory)*

Dr. Jordan Davis MD- Toxic studies Institute in Boca Raton is quoted as saying "Walking into the average dental office can result in a mercury exposure that is equivalent to having 19 amalgam fillings".

HOW CAN I FIND OUT IF I AM MERCURY TOXIC?

How can you find out how much mercury you have in your body? (Numbness and tingling, paralysis, tremors and pain are just some of the symptoms of chronic metal intoxication associated with the use of mercury dental amalgams.) Your mercury load will not be found in a blood sample. Only a very recent exposure would show up in blood. The mercury will quickly bind to tissues in organs and no longer be circulating in the blood stream.

An accurate test is the DMPS challenge in which a base line 24 hour urine mercury level is checked. This 1st unchallenged 24 hour collection shows what your body is excreting on a daily basis, **not what your total load is**. Then a physician administers a chelating agent that binds to mercury allowing it to be excreted. The amount of mercury excreted in this urine (measuring micrograms of mercury) or your feces (new research shows Grams of mercury are passed) indicates the amount in your body.[20] [21]

Another test that is used is a hair analysis. This is a good test if you want to know what is being excreted, but like the first 24 hour urine it will not tell you what the load is. It is possible to show up with low to no mercury and after a chelating agent is used and the sample retaken a huge increase is now seen. The disadvantage to using hair is that your sample takes so long to grow to be able to harvest accurate results.

It is possible for a person to have mercury in body tissues and not have any silver fillings in their mouth. Mercury passes through the placental barrier, so a mother with amalgam fillings may pass mercury to her unborn child. This child will now have mercury in its body tissues even though he/she has never had a silver filling.

Dr. Hal Huggins DDS was a pioneer in bringing the

amalgam filling and mercury toxicity issue to the attention of the general public.

Based on the information from Dr. Hal Huggins book, "*It's All In Your Head*"

The following are considered chemical indicators of mercury toxicity:

* A white blood cell count above 7,500 or below 4,500.

* Hematocrit above 50 percent or below 40 percent (this is the percentage by volume of packed red blood cells in a sample of blood after it has been spun in a centrifuge).

* A lymphocyte count above 2,800 or below 1,800 (lymphocytes are a type of white blood cell that function in the development of the immune system.)

* A blood protein level above 7.5 grams per 100 milliliters of serum (7.5 g percent ml).

* A blood triglyceride level above 150 mg percent ml.

* A blood urea nitrogen (BUN) level above 18 or below 12 percent

* A level of nickel in the hair above 1.5 parts per million (ppm).

* A hair aluminum level above 15 ppm.

* A hair manganese level below 0.3 ppm.

* Immune reactions to aluminum, nickel, mercury, copper, or gold.

Dr. Huggins writes in his new book "Uninformed Consent" that the newer high Copper Mercury amalgams actually leach Mercury out at a faster rate.

The next few pages from the Texas State Department of Health and from the Material Safety Data Sheet on amalgams, details the health hazards of mercury.

Texas Department of Health

Division of Occupational Health

1100 West 49th Street
Austin, Texas 78756
(512) 834-6600 ext. 2452
(800) 452-2791 ext. 2452

Elemental Mercury Fact Sheet

What Is Mercury?

Mercury is a chemical element that occurs naturally in the environment and is used in several industrial activities. The three primary chemical forms of mercury are elemental (metallic), inorganic salts, and organic mercury. Metallic mercury can be found as a shiny silver liquid, a fine droplet mist, and an odorless vapor. Common articles containing elemental mercury are the traditional thermometer and blood pressure-measuring device found in a doctor's office.

How Might I Be Exposed to Elemental Mercury?

Everyone is exposed to very low levels of mercury from the air, water, and diet. Dental fillings, made from a combination of silver and mercury, slowly release mercury vapors and can also be absorbed by the body. Some traditional hispanic and oriental cultures use liquid mercury in folk remedies. Metallic mercury fumes can be produced environmentally by spills, hazardous waste handling facilities, or plants that burn fossil fuels such as coal.

However, many workers may be exposed to this toxic metal from occupational sources. Most on the job exposures are the result of breathing air containing mercury fumes. Metallic mercury is used in several industrial purposes like chemical, battery, and electrical equipment manufacturing. This liquid metal is a vital component of engineering and scientific instruments that measure pressure. Elemental mercury is frequently associated with the dental, gold mining, and salvage industries. Indirectly, the families of workers in these industries may be exposed to mercury from contaminated work-related articles and clothing.

How Does Elemental Mercury Enter and Leave the Body?

Mercury can easily enter the body through the lungs as air containing the metallic vapor is breathed. This vapor readily enters the bloodstream and is carried throughout the body, but is mainly deposited in the nervous tissues and kidneys. Metallic mercury can be absorbed through the skin, but poorly enters the body from the digestive system. Over a period of weeks or months mercury accumulated in the body is slowly eliminated. The mercury can leave the body in urine, feces, and by the breath.

How Can Elemental Mercury Affect My Health?

The nervous system is very sensitive to the toxic effects of mercury. The undue exposure of the brain to elemental mercury may produce personality changes and impairment of vision, hearing, or memory. Common personality changes observed with elevated exposure may be nervousness, irritability, reduced self-confidence, loss of appetite, and sleep disturbances. Symptoms such as nervous muscle shakes and loss of nerve to muscle coordination have been reported in workers exposed to mercury vapors over long periods of time.

Health effects like nausea, vomiting, diarrhea, skin rashes, and eye irritation have been noted in acute cases (high-level exposures over a short time interval). Lung damage, increased heart rate, higher blood pressure, and even coma are other severe problems seen with acute exposure.

The kidneys are also sensitive to the effects of elemental mercury, for they are a primary site of its concentration and elimination from the body.

Is There a Medical Test to Determine Whether I Have Been Exposed to Elemental Mercury?

There are accurate and reliable methods, available to your doctor, that measure mercury levels in the body. Urine and blood samples can be collected for testing in a medical laboratory to evaluate mercury exposure. A blood mercury test may be useful in specific acute cases and when taken minutes after the exposure. However, 24-hour urine or spot samples are the most effective tools to measure long-term occupational exposure.

Public Health Summary

Exposure to elevated levels of elemental mercury for extended periods can permanently damage the brain, kidneys, and developing fetus. For this reason, it is important to recognize the above symptoms as possible signs of excessive mercury exposure, and seek appropriate medical assistance.

Some format and content of this fact sheet are drawn from the "Public Health Statement" in the *Toxicological Profile for Mercury*, Agency for Toxic Substances and Disease Registry, Public Health Service, 1994. DOH Toxic. Act./ circa 4/95

62

NIOSH

A Recommended Standard for Occupational Exposure to.....

Inorganic Mercury

The criteria document for protection from exposure to inorganic mercury has been prepared in accordance with sections 6(b)(7) and 20(a)(3) of the Occupational Safety and Health Act and was transmitted to the Occupational Safety and Health Administration, (OSHA), U.S. Department of Labor, August 13, 1973, for review and consideration in the standard setting process.

The standard is based upon criteria developed from the results of investigations of the effects inorganic mercury has on the central nervous system. The criteria document proposed is a complete criteria document and includes environmental and medical monitoring. Exposure to inorganic mercury occurs in many industries, such as chemical and drug syntheses, hospitals, laboratories, dental practice, instrument manufacture, and battery manufacture. It is estimated that approximately 150,000 workers are exposed to mercury.

The recommendation for occupational exposure to inorganic mercury takes into consideration information and research data on health effects and limited data on technical feasibility.

The criteria document was reviewed by nine knowledgeable consultants and two professional societies. There were three responses from solicitation in the *Federal Register*.

There is some reason to believe that inorganic and organic mercury compounds (except methyl and ethyl compounds) are slightly less toxic than mercury vapor, but the standard proposed is the same for all these non-alkyl forms of mercury. There are difficulties in distinguishing between the several forms by available sampling and analytical methods, and there is reason to believe that these non-alkyl forms may be in part interconvertible in air or in sampling apparatus. Thus, it was concluded that the same environmental limit (0.05 mg Hg/cu m) should apply to all forms of mercury other than short-chain alkyl forms.

It was the reviewers' belief that the standard proposed is appropriate and that there is no additional information now available that would affect the standard. As a result of comments from reviewers, the environmental standard was reduced from 0.1 mg Hg/cu m, as a ceiling, to 0.05 mg Hg/cu m as a time-weighted average.

The following is the first chapter of the criteria document. It contains the NIOSH recommendations for controlling worker exposure to inorganic mercury.

U. S. DEPARTMENT OF HEALTH, EDUCATION, AND WELFARE
Public Health Service
Center for Disease Control
National Institute for Occupational Safety and Health

1. RECOMMENDATIONS FOR AN INORGANIC MERCURY STANDARD

The National Institute for Occupational Safety and Health recommends that employee exposure to inorganic mercury in the workplace be controlled by adherence to the following sections. The standard is designed to protect the health and safety of workers for an 8-hour day, 40-hour week over a working lifetime. Compliance with the standard should prevent adverse effects of inorganic mercury on the health and safety of workers. The standard is measurable by techniques that are valid, reproducible, and available to industry and governmental agencies and is attainable with existing technology. The criteria and the standard recommended in this document will be reviewed and revised as necessary.

"Inorganic mercury" in this document includes elemental mercury, and all inorganic mercury compounds and organic mercury compounds other than ethyl and methyl mercury compounds.

"Exposure to inorganic mercury" is defined as exposure to a concentration of inorganic mercury greater than 40% of the recommended level in the workplace. Exposure at lower environmental concentrations will not require adherence to the following sections, except Section 7a.

Section 1 — Environmental (Workplace air)

(a) Concentration
Occupational exposure to mercury shall be controlled so that workers are not exposed to inorganic mercury at a concentration greater than 0.05 mg Hg/cu m determined as a time-weighted average (TWA) exposure for an 8-hour workday.

(b) Sampling and Analysis
Procedures for collection of environmental samples shall be as provided in Appendix I, or by a method shown to be equivalent. Analysis of samples shall be as provided in Appendix II, or by any method shown to be equivalent in sensitivity, accuracy, and precision.

Section 2 — Medical

Comprehensive medical examinations (which should include complete urinalysis) shall be made available to all workers subject to "exposure to inorganic mercury" prior to employee placement and annually thereafter. These examinations should place emphasis on any symptoms or signs of unacceptable mercury absorption such as loss of weight, sleeplessness, tremors, personality change, or other evidence of central nervous system involvement.

Medical records shall be available to the medi-

cal representatives of the employer, of the Secretary of Labor, of the Secretary of Health, Education, and Welfare, and of the employee at his request. These records shall be kept for at least five years after the employee's last occupational exposure to inorganic mercury.

Section 3 — Labeling (Posting)

The following warning shall be posted to be readily visible at or near entrances or accessways to work areas where there is potential exposure to inorganic mercury.

WARNING!

MERCURY WORK AREA

Unauthorized Persons Not Permitted

The following warning shall be posted in readily visible locations in any work area where there is potential exposure to inorganic mercury.

WARNING!

MERCURY

High Concentrations

Are Hazardous to Health

Maintain Adequate Ventilation.

If environmental levels are at or greater than the recommended standard, add information to the warning describing the location of the respirators.

These warnings shall be printed in English and in the predominant primary language of non-English-speaking workers, if any.

Section 4 — Personal Protective Equipment and Work Clothing

Subsections (a) and (b) shall apply whenever a variance from the standard recommended in Section 1 is granted under provisions of the Occupational Safety and Health Act, or in the interim period during the application for a variance. When the limits of exposure to inorganic mercury prescribed in paragraph (a) of Section 1 cannot be met by limiting the concentration of mercury in the work environment, an employer must utilize a program of respiratory protection to effect the required protection of every worker exposed.

(a) Respiratory Protection

Engineering controls shall be used wherever feasible to maintain inorganic mercury concentrations in the workplace air at or below the prescribed limits. Appropriate respirators, as prescribed in Table I-1, shall be provided and used when a variance has been granted to allow respirators as a means of control of routine operations and while the application is pending. Administrative controls can also be used to reduce exposure. Respirators shall also be provided and used for nonroutine operations (occasional brief exposures above the environmental standard and for emergencies); however, for these instances, a

(3) A respiratory protective program meeting the general requirements outlined in section 3.5 of American National Standard for Respiratory Protection Z88.2-1969 shall be established and enforced by the employer.

(4) The employer shall provide respirators in accordance with Table I-1 and shall ensure that the employee uses the appropriate respirator.

(5) Respiratory protective devices described in Table I-1 shall be either those approved under 30 CFR 11, published March 25, 1972, or under the following regulations.

(A) Gas masks — 30 CFR 13 (Bureau of Mines Schedule 14 E)

(B) Self-contained breathing apparatus — 30 CFR 11 (Bureau of Mines Schedule 13 E)

Table I-1

Requirements for Respirator Usage

At Concentrations Above the Standard

Mg Hg/cu m	Respirator Type*
Less than 5.0	I, II, III
Greater than 5.0	II, III

*TYPE I - Full facepiece gas mask equipped with a high efficiency filter plus canister containing iodine-impregnated charcoal.

TYPE II - Type C (positive pressure) supplied air respirator.

TYPE III - (Positive pressure) self-contained breathing apparatus.

variance is not required but the requirements set forth below continue to apply. Respirators shall only be used pursuant to the following requirements:

(1) For the purpose of determining the class of respirator to be used, the employer shall measure the atmospheric concentration of inorganic mercury in the workplace when the initial application for variance is made and thereafter whenever process, worksite, climate or control changes occur which are likely to affect the mercury concentration. The employer shall ensure that no worker is exposed to inorganic mercury in excess of the standard because of improper respirator selection or fit.

(2) Employees experiencing breathing difficulty while using respirators shall be evaluated by a physician to determine the ability of the worker to wear a respirator.

(C) Supplied air respirator — 30 CFR 12 (Bureau of Mines Schedule 19 B)

(6) Usage of a respirator specified for use in higher concentrations of inorganic mercury is permitted in atmospheres of lower concentrations.

(b) Work clothing

(1) Each employee subject to exposure to inorganic mercury shall be provided coveralls or similar full body work clothing, shoes or shoe covers, and hat, which shall be worn during the working hours in areas where there is exposure to inorganic mercury. A daily change of clean work clothing shall be supplied by the employer.

(2) Adequate shower facilities provided with hot and cold or tempered water shall be available for use and used by workers.

(3) Work and street clothing shall not be stored in the same locker.

(4) Work clothing should be vacuumed before removal. Clothes shall not be cleaned by blowing or shaking.

Section 5 — Appraisal of Employees of Hazards from Inorganic Mercury

(a) Each employee exposed to inorganic mercury shall be apprised at the beginning of his employment or assignment to an inorganic mercury work area of hazards, relevant symptoms, appropriate emergency procedures, and proper conditions and precautions for safe use or exposure. He shall be instructed as to availability of such information including that prescribed in (b) below. Such information shall be kept on file and shall be accessible to the worker at each place of employment where inorganic mercury is used.

(b) Information as specified in Appendix III shall be recorded on U.S. Department of Labor Form OSHA-20, "Material Safety Data Sheet" (see Appendix III) or on a similar form approved by the Occupational Safety and Health Administration, U.S. Department of Labor.

Section 6 — Work Practices

(a) Emergency Procedures

(1) Procedures, including fire fighting procedures, shall be established and implemented to meet foreseeable emergency events.

(2) Respirators shall be available for wearing during emergencies. Self-contained respirators shall be available for employee use in the event of fire or other emergencies where equipment or operations cannot be abandoned because of an emergency.

(b) Exhaust Systems

Where a local exhaust ventilation system is used, it shall be designed and maintained to prevent the accumulation or recirculation of mercury vapor, dust, and fumes into the workroom.

(c) General Housekeeping

(1) Floors, work surfaces, and equipment shall be so constructed and maintained as not to have cracks, crevices, or other areas which may retain mercury.

(2) Spills and leaks of mercury shall be promptly cleaned up either mechanically or chemically, or by other appropriate means. No blowing or dry sweeping shall be permitted. When vacuum cleaners are used, they shall be equipped with mercury vapor absorbing filters to prevent dispersal of mercury vapors into the workplace air and shall be maintained so they will not disperse mercury-laden dust into the workplace.

(3) Waste mercury or materials contaminated with mercury shall be kept in vaporproof containers, under water, or in chemically treated solutions, pending removal for disposal or processing for reuse.

(d) General Procedures

(1) Containers of mercury shall be kept covered when it is not necessary to have them open for process operations.

(2) Open containers of mercury, to the greatest extent possible, shall have the surface of the mercury covered with an aqueous layer maintained at a temperature below its boiling point to prevent vaporization of the mercury.

Section 7 — Sanitation Practices

(a) Food preparation, dispensing (including vending machines), and eating shall be prohibited in mercury work areas.

(b) Smoking materials shall not be permitted in mercury work areas.

(c) Handwashing facilities, including hot and cold running water, soap, and towels, shall be made available adjacent to mercury work areas. Employees shall be instructed in the importance of thoroughly washing their hands before eating or smoking.

(d) Soiled clothing shall be stored in vaporproof containers pending removal for laundering.

(e) Laundering of work clothing shall be provided by the employer. Persons responsible for laundering mercury contaminated clothing shall be informed of the hazards involved.

Section 8 — Monitoring and Recordkeeping Requirements

Workroom areas where it has been determined, on the basis of an industrial hygiene survey or the judgment of a compliance officer, that environmental levels do not exceed 40% of the environmental standard shall not be considered to involve worker exposure to inorganic mercury. An additional survey shall be made if there is a change in process or engineering controls. Records of these surveys, including the basis for concluding that air levels are below 40% of the environmental standard, shall be kept.

Requirements set forth below apply to inorganic mercury exposures.

(a) Employers shall monitor environmental levels of inorganic mercury at least every 6 months. Breathing zone samples shall be collected to permit calculation of a time-weighted average exposure for every operation.

(b) When any time-weighted average exposure is at or above the environmental standard, immediate steps shall be taken to reduce environmental levels. Samples shall be taken every 30 days until the environmental level has been reduced below the standard.

66

MATERIAL SAFETY DATA SHEET

U.S. DEPARTMENT OF LABOR
Occupational Safety and Health Administration

Form Approved
OMB No. 44-R1387

Required under USDL Safety and Health Regulations for Ship Repairing,
Shipbuilding, and Shipbreaking (29 CFR 1915, 1916, 1917)

SECTION I

Distributor: GENERAL REFINERIES, INC.
7227 NORTH HAMLIN AVENUE, SKOKIE, ILLINOIS 60076

MANUFACTURER'S NAME
D.F. GOLDSMITH CHEMICAL & METAL CORP.

EMERGENCY TELEPHONE NO
312 869-7800

ADDRESS (Number, Street, City, State and Zip Code)
909 Pitner Ave., Evanston, Ill. 60202

CHEMICAL NAME AND SYNONYMS
MERCURY (QUICKSILVER)

TRADE NAME AND SYNONYMS
DFG MERCURY (SPECTROMERC)

CHEMICAL FAMILY

FORMULA

SECTION II — HAZARDOUS INGREDIENTS

PAINTS, PRESERVATIVES & SOLVENTS	%	TLV (Units)	ALLOYS AND METALLIC COATINGS	%	TLV (Units)
PIGMENTS			BASE METAL Mercury	.10	mg/M
CATALYST			ALLOYS		
VEHICLE			METALLIC COATINGS		
SOLVENTS			FILLER METAL PLUS COATING OR CORE FLUX		
ADDITIVES			OTHERS		
OTHERS					

HAZARDOUS MIXTURES OF OTHER LIQUIDS, SOLIDS, OR GASES				%	TLV (Units)
N/A					

*8 hour weighted average time

SECTION III — PHYSICAL DATA

BOILING POINT (°F)	356.9C	SPECIFIC GRAVITY (H_2O=1)	13.546
VAPOR PRESSURE (mm Hg)	0.0019	PERCENT, VOLATILE BY VOLUME (%)	100
VAPOR DENSITY (AIR=1)	1.015	EVAPORATION RATE (=1)	Less than one
SOLUBILITY IN WATER	nil		
APPEARANCE AND ODOR	SILVERY, ODORLESS LIQUID AT ROOM TEMPERATURE		

SECTION IV — FIRE AND EXPLOSION HAZARD DATA

			LEL	UEL
FLASH POINT (Method used) N/A	FLAMMABLE LIMITS			
EXTINGUISHING MEDIA N/A				
SPECIAL FIRE FIGHTING PROCEDURES N/A				
UNUSUAL FIRE AND EXPLOSION HAZARDS N/A				

SECTION V - HEALTH HAZARD DATA Page 49

TIME SHOLD LIMIT VALUE	Avoid prolonged breathing of vapor & ingestion.
EFFECTS OF OVEREXPOSURE	Muscle tremors, loosening of teeth, mental aberrations, possible death.
AGENCY AND FIRST AID PROCEDURES	Contact qualified Physician. If ingested, DO NOT INDUCE VOMITING. Eye contact, wash with water. Skin contact, wash with standard soap & water. Avoide skin contact. Wear protective clothing.

SECTION VI — REACTIVITY DATA

STABILITY		CONDITIONS TO AVOID
	UNSTABLE	Avoid long exposure to air, heat and non-ferrous metals.
	STABLE	
INCOMPATABILITY (Materials to avoid)		None-ferrous metals
HAZARDOUS DECOMPOSITION PRODUCTS		Mercury Vapor
HAZARDOUS POLYMERIZATION	MAY OCCUR	N/A
	WILL NOT OCCUR	N/A

CONDITIONS TO AVOID

SECTION VII - SPILL OR LEAK PROCEDURES

STEPS TO BE TAKEN IN CASE MATERIAL IS RELEASED OR SPILLED	Use under well-ventillated conditions, sweep spills promptly (using special vacuum cleaner if possible)., use sulfur-bearing weeping compound.
DISPOSAL METHOD	DO NOT INCINERATE - return to reclamation centers.

HARRY J. BOSWORTH CO.

SECTION VIII — SPECIAL PROTECTION INFORMATION

RESPIRATORY PROTECTION (Specify type)		Should be NIOSH-MESA certified	
VENTILATION	LOCAL EXHAUST	Yes, point of origin	SPECIAL
	MECHANICAL (General)	Yes	OTHER
PROTECTIVE GLOVES	Yes		EYE PROTECTION Yes - glasses
OTHER PROTECTIVE EQUIPMENT	Aprons, rubber soled shoes, clothing changes suggested.		

SECTION IX — SPECIAL PRECAUTIONS

PRECAUTIONS TO BE TAKEN IN HANDLING AND STORING	Always keep mercury stored in a sealed container away from heat.
OTHER PRECAUTIONS	

PAGE (2)

GPO 9 34 1 99

Form OSHA-20
Rev. May 72

68

OTHER HEAVY METALS

What about other heavy metals? Many people react to nickel. Nickel is commonly used in crowns and bridges.[22] A high number of people are sensitive to nickel. This is why so many women can not wear cheap earrings. The high nickel content bothers them. California's Proposition 65 applies to nickel too. Nickel is known to cause cancer and birth defects; it has the ability to bind to Oxygen, Nitrogen and Sulpher containing biochemicals. Nickel is immunosuppressive and inactivates the natural killer cells. Nickel can attack the visual areas of the brain. Nickel is usually mixed with chromium and cobalt. Remember the law does not prohibit exposure, but requires the patient be informed.

Copper increases the carcinogenic activity of nickel. The newer silver fillings are higher in copper and cause the mercury to be emitted 50% faster than the older amalgams. Copper is in 90% of dental golds.

Occasionally, thallium and geranium are found together in amalgam tooth fillings.

In order to prevent using a dental material that may cause problems, find a biological dentist. These dentists can have you tested to learn what dental materials are suitable for you. This testing can be done by blood testing (Clifford Laboratories), Electro-Dermal Screening (EDS) or Applied Kinesiology (AK). You still need to interview the office. Just because someone is a member does not mean they do things the way you want them done. Take responsibility!

Should everyone have their mercury amalgams removed? You can not find a dentist that will recommend you have amalgams removed and replaced for health reasons, because the State Boards of Dentistry in most every state have passed rulings on that topic. A dentist that diagnoses removal of functioning, non-decayed restorations, solely for the replacement of those mercury fillings with composite fillings, may *lose his license*. Now, <u>you</u> can read about mercury, make an educated decision and request the amalgams all be replaced. Then the state boards have no jurisdiction in the matter. Physicians trained in alternative medicine are not too hasty in recommending that the amalgams need to be removed and replaced either. It is more common for the physician to recommend you not have any new amalgams placed. The physician can test you to see if heavy metal toxicity is a problem for you on an individual basis. This is best done with a physician trained in chelation therapy.

If you decide to replace your amalgams with another type of filling, it is **imperative** that you consult a dentist trained in the proper protocol. There are strict guidelines to follow in terms of proper amalgam removal: use of a rubber dam, use of supplemental air via a nosepiece, protective equipment for both the patient and the dental personnel, heavy duty suction, air filtering system and detox measures. A dentist trained in safe removal of the mercury will quarter the filling and remove it in large pieces to reduce the amount of vapor caused by drilling. They will use chlorella rinses during the procedure. Chlorella is an algae known for its ability to bind to heavy metals.

Remember that the vapor form of mercury is the most toxic and absorbable form. Improper removal of amalgam fillings may put you at a higher risk of mercury toxicity due to inhalation of the vapors created during the drilling process.[23] There could be great risks in your health by removing amalgams improperly. Removal is not recommended during pregnancy or nursing as mercury is excreted in the milk.

More About The Toxic Effects Of Heavy Metals

1.7 WHAT RECOMMENDATIONS HAS THE FEDERAL GOVERNMENT MADE TO PROTECT HUMAN HEALTH?

The National Institute for Occupational Safety and Health (NIOSH) recommends a standard for occupational exposure of 0.5 µg beryllium/m^3 of workroom air during an 8-hour shift to protect workers from a concern that beryllium may cause cancer. The Occupational Safety and Health Administration (OSHA) has set a limit of 2 µg beryllium/m^3 of workroom air for an 8-hour work shift. The Environmental Protection Agency restricts the amount of beryllium emitted into the environment by industries that process beryllium ores, metal, oxide, alloys, or waste to 10 grams (g) in a 24-hour period, or to an amount that would result in atmospheric levels of 0.01 µg beryllium/m^3 of air, averaged over a 30-day period. For more information, please read Chapter 7.

1.8 WHERE CAN I GET MORE INFORMATION?

If you have any more questions or concerns, please contact your community or state health or environmental quality department or:

> Agency for Toxic Substances and Disease Registry
> Division of Toxicology
> 1600 Clifton Road NE, E-29
> Atlanta, Georgia 30333

This agency can also provide you with information on the location of the nearest occupational and environmental health clinic. These clinics specialize in the recognition, evaluation, and treatment of illnesses resulting from exposure to hazardous substances.

93

5. POTENTIAL FOR HUMAN EXPOSURE

5.4.4 Other Environmental Media

Several foodstuffs from New South Wales, Australia, were analyzed, and the following average beryllium concentrations were found (in pg/kg fresh weight): beans (0.065); cabbage (0.234); hen eggs yolk and whites (0.061); milk (0.166); mushrooms (1.58); edible nuts (0.21–0.52); tomatoes (0.21); crabs (15.4–26.2); fish fillets (0.16–1.48); oyster flesh (0.6–2.0); and scallops (0.34) (Meehan and Smythe 1967). The following beryllium concentrations (µg/kg dry weight) were reported in West German food samples: polished rice (80); toasted bread (120); potatoes (170); tomatoes (240); and green head lettuce (330) (Reeves 1986). The reported beryllium concentrations (µg/kg dry weight) in crops from Egypt were as follows: eggplant (370); potatoes (300); green pepper (400); kidney bean (2,500); garden pea (430); vegetable marrow (400); pear (400); lettuce (600); dill (420); and parsley (400) (Awadallah et al. 1986).

The beryllium concentrations, expressed in fresh weight, in both raw carrots and field corn grown in the United States were <25 pg/kg, with a sample detection limit of 25 µg/kg (Wolnik et al. 1984). The beryllium concentration in tissue of bottom fish (English sole, _Parophrys vetulus_) caught in Commencement Bay, Tacoma, Washington, was 6 µg/kg (Nicola et al. 1987). If a factor of 10 is used for conversion of fresh weight to dry weight, it is apparent that the beryllium levels in the German and Egyptian crops that were sampled are higher by at least two orders of magnitude than the beryllium levels in the Australian crops. The discrepancy may result from errors in the method used for the determination of beryllium, the lower levels of environmental contamination of Australian food, or a possible combination of both.

The beryllium levels in the sediments of Lake Pontchartrain, Louisiana, were 0.05–0.5 mg/kg (dry weight) (Byrne and DeLeon 1986). In sediments of the Detroit River and western basin of Lake Erie, the levels were 0.1–3.8 mg/kg (dry weight) (Lum and Gammon 1985).

Beryllium has been detected in U.S. orchard leaves and in various trees and shrubs at concentrations of 26 µg/kg and ≤1 mg/kg, respectively (IARC 1980).

Beryllium levels of 0.47–0.74 µg/cigarette have been detected in three brands of West German cigarettes; 2–10% of the beryllium was found in the cigarette smoke (Reeves 1986).

5.5 GENERAL POPULATION AND OCCUPATIONAL EXPOSURE

The general population is exposed to trace amounts of beryllium by inhalation of air and ingestion of drinking water and food. If the average concentration of beryllium in air is assumed to be 0.03 ng/m³ (see Section 5.4.1), and it is further assumed that a normal U.S. adult inhales 20 m³ of air per day, the daily inhalation exposure to beryllium for a U.S. adult would be 0.0006 µg. Similarly, if the concentration of beryllium in average U.S. drinking water is 0.2 µg/L (see Section 5.4.2), and the consumption rate of drinking water by a normal adult is assumed to be 2 L/day, the daily exposure from drinking water would be 0.4 µg. Reliable data regarding the daily exposure rate to beryllium from food consumption are lacking. It has been estimated that the daily intake of beryllium from U.S. food is 0.12 µg (EPA 1987). This estimate is based on an arbitrary value for beryllium content of a total diet sample of 0.1 ng/g and a daily consumption of 1,200 g of food (EPA 1987). Other investigators have reported the total daily intake of beryllium to range from 10 to 20 µg of which ~12 µg is contributed by food. These values, however, are approximated and need to be verified (Tsalev and Zaprianov 1984).

People who work in industries where beryllium is present have a greater probability of inhalation exposure than nonoccupational groups. The estimated daily-weighted average beryllium exposure levels for some workers in

72

94

5. POTENTIAL FOR HUMAN EXPOSURE

a plant that extracted and produced the metal were >50 $\mu g/m^3$ during the mid-1960s; the levels were >30 $\mu g/m^3$ during the mid-1970s. After 1977, the plant complied with the permissible exposure limit of 2.0 $\mu g/m^3$ (Kriebel et al. 1988). The time-weighted average personal air concentration for beryllium in a precious metal refinery in 1983 ranged from 0.22 to 42.3 $\mu g/m^3$ (Cullen et al. 1987). Determination of beryllium concentrations in the lungs at autopsy of deceased German mine workers revealed 2.3–34 times higher lung levels than in an unexposed control group (Baumgardt et al. 1986). It is likely that dental technicians who work with beryllium-containing dental alloys without using appropriate handling safeguards may be exposed to higher levels of beryllium than the normal population (Bauer et al. 1988).

A National Occupational Exposure Survey conducted by NIOSH during 1981–1983 estimated that 13,869 workers were potentially exposed to beryllium metal and 4,305 workers to beryllium oxide in the workplace (NIOSH 1989a).

5.6 POPULATIONS WITH POTENTIALLY HIGH EXPOSURES

Several populations are at high risk for beryllium exposure. Individuals with the highest risk include people who are occupationally exposed to beryllium from manufacturing, fabricating, or reclaiming industries; however, there have been no reports of disease attributable to beryllium exposure as a result of beryllium ore mining operations, (Eisenbud and Lisson 1983; EPA 1987; Hamilton and Hardy 1974). People living near beryllium-emitting industries may be at a slightly increased risk of beryllium exposure due to contact with beryllium-contaminated dust within the household, as opposed to ambient air levels. Occupationally exposed workers who carry beryllium dust on their clothes from the workplace to their home may increase the risk of beryllium exposure to their family members (EPA 1987). However, it is common today for beryllium industries to provide and launder employee's work clothes. The National Emission Standard for Hazardous Air Pollutants restricts the amount of beryllium emitted into the environment by industries that process beryllium ores, metals, oxides, alloys, or wastes to 10 g in a 24-hour period (EPA 1982). No new cases of beryllium disease in people living near beryllium-processing industries have been reported in the past several years, probably because the past exposures were relatively high compared to present levels of beryllium in the ambient and workplace air (EPA 1987).

Smokers may inhale unusually high concentrations of beryllium. Based on an analysis of West German cigarettes and smoke (Reeves 1986), an average of 35 ng of beryllium may be inhaled per cigarette. A person smoking one pack of cigarettes each day would inhale ~700 ng of beryllium, which is nearly twice the daily consumption from other sources (EPA 1987). This estimate depends on the amount of beryllium contained in the native tobacco leaf, and it may vary depending on the source of tobacco.

It is also possible that certain individuals may be exposed to higher than normal beryllium from implanted dental prostheses, although no studies on beryllium leaching from dental prostheses are available (EPA 1987). The mantles of some lanterns used by campers contain ~600 μg of beryllium, and most of the beryllium becomes airborne during the first 15 minutes when a new mantle is used (Fishbein 1981). Therefore, people who camp outdoors and use these mantles are possibly exposed to higher than normal levels of beryllium. A small percentage of the population is sensitive to very low concentrations of beryllium, but there is no evidence that sensitivity develops at beryllium concentrations present in food or water, or that sensitivity is aggravated by ingestion of beryllium. No other special groups at risk were identified EPA (1980).

5.7 ADEQUACY OF THE DATABASE

Section 104(i)(5) of CERCLA directs the Administrator of ATSDR (in consultation with the Administrator of EPA and agencies and programs of the Public Health Service) to assess whether adequate information on the health

73

GALVANISM

Two or more dissimilar metals (for instance dental gold and mercury) act as electrodes, with saliva serving as an electrolyte; creating a battery. The saliva in the mouth is electrically conductive due to its mineral content. This results in an electrical current that is strong enough to cause a number of problems. These electrical currents between various metals in and on the teeth and dental prosthesis cause irritations in the nervous system. Many therapy resistant conditions are responsive to replacement of old metal fillings. The diagnosis of galvanism can be made using a device that measures oral electric currents called an electro galvanometer.

There are two types of electrical activity on the surface of a filling. One is just like a regular battery, called bimetallic. Bimetallic activity happens when two or more dissimilar metals are in an electrolyte solution that conducts electricity. This bimetallic activity will produce a current or a flow of electrons. The other type of electrical activity is called differential aeration. This occurs between saliva and areas that contain different amounts of oxygen. This can be seen in the saliva covering a filling, because there is less oxygen than the saliva on the top of unrestored enamel. This differential aeration thus produces a current.

What is considered a high current in the mouth? Reinhold Voll, M.D., of Germany, recommends against the presence of more than 4 microamps of current. Dental gold and amalgam placed side by side in the mouth, may act as an electric element producing a voltage of 1000 millivolts or more. Elevations of current readings may be seen with amalgam to steel, gold to steel and other metals. These voltage build-ups close to the base of the skull are certainly not without consequence to the patient. What is the direct result of sending electrical currents into the tissue near the brain? Because of the ongoing and constant electrical current burdening the person, there is difficulty in regulation. Such currents can disturb the bioenergetic equilibrium to a considerable extent and cause electrolytic effects on the dental material. This usually shows up as corrosion of the metal in the mouth. This corrosion results in a constant stream of metal ions dragged into the person where they develop into allergic or pathogenic disturbances.[24] This is seen in the gold or amalgam filling as pitting with some oxidation. If you have gold and silver fillings you may notice that the silver fillings are not shiny. They are dark gray to black in color due to the oxidation.

Metals, specifically their ions, have varying "affinities" to certain tissues in the human body. Mercury will migrate to the brain, joints and kidneys. Beryllium was, or still is included in some dental alloys. It will deposit in the liver and kidneys. Until recently many dental solders contained cadmium. In addition, cadmium is also found in the red color of some partial and denture plastics. The large surface area in contact with the mucous tissues presents a constant source of intoxication to the body. Now that the teratrogenous (cancer causing) effects of this heavy metal are more widely known, it is hoped to condemn solders and dyes containing cadmium. Cadmium accumulates in the liver and kidneys. Nickel deposits in the skin, the central nervous system, and in the lungs and kidneys.[25]

Since fluids containing minerals are found in the teeth, the mouth, and the bone, there are a variety of directions that the electrical current can go. Tooth to muscle, tooth to joint or even tooth to part of the brain.

Electro galvanism can cause a lack of concentration and memory, insomnia, ringing in the ears, vertigo, epilepsy, hearing loss and eye problems. Signs and symptoms of galvanism are: headaches, dizziness, metallic taste in mouth, fainting spells, nausea, burning sensation to tongue and dry mouth.[26] [27] [28] Some people with these symptoms see physicians and are placed on medications. Some medications may relieve the symptoms. Removal of the material and replacement with a more biocompatible material is indicated.[29] This may be a better option than long term use of medications that have side effects.

CHAPTER SEVEN

DENTAL APPLIANCES AND RESTORATIONS

ORTHODONTIC APPLIANCES

Here we have the issue of another metal,(stainless steel) that contains high levels of nickel. It has been shown statistically that about 14% of women and 6% of men are allergic or sensitive to nickel.[30] Remember, if you have any other metals in your mouth, there is the electro galvanic issue to deal with. Ever hear of something as bizarre as, a person with a mouth full of braces being able to pick up a radio station? The length of the arch wire is a great length for an antenna.

Now we bring another problem into the light. Metal crossing the midline of the body. It is a fact that the right side of your brain directs the left side of your body and the left side of your brain directs the right side of your body. When a stroke patient has a left side deficit, you know the damage is on the right side of the brain. In contrast, acupuncture points on one side of the body relate to organs on that side of the body, *there are a few exceptions*. As metal crosses the midline of the body, it is acting as an antenna and false messages are sent or messages get scrambled. This can be demonstrated with Applied Kinesiology and a pair of metal framed glasses. The metal across the bridge of the nose, in the frame of the eyeglass, is just like the arch wire of braces and the orthodontic ligature wires that cross over the middle of the mouth. The metal provides a detour for the flow of energy that the body is generating throughout the meridians. This is also seen in patients that wear full or partial dentures containing metal that crosses the center of the mouth. Some people will even tell you "I can't wait to get home in the evening to take my partial out."[31] This can also be seen with heavy metal necklaces, where the owner actually feels better as the jewelry is removed.

In many cases orthodontics may be necessary to improve the relationship of the teeth to each other. During the treatment period it may be helpful to use a metal detoxification program through a qualified physician to prevent metals from settling into tissues and thereby damaging organs. After the treatment is done and the need for a retainer arises, ask the orthodontist to make a plastic one instead of the traditional wire that is cemented to the tongue side of the bottom front teeth. This wire is usually high in nickel and crosses the midline.[32] [33] New nickel free materials are available through Orthodontic Express 1-800-547-2669.

COMPOSITE FILLINGS

The white fillings are usually composite resin in nature. These can be made of glass ions, plastics or other synthetic materials. Some even contain ions of metals to increase the crushing strength, making them more durable.

The preparation of the tooth by the dentist for a composite filling is quite different than that for an amalgam filling. The amalgam filling does not stick to the tooth. The space created by the dentist to receive the amalgam may be made with slanted walls, so that the bottom opening of the hole is wider than the top opening of the hole. This beveled effect acts as a retention wall to keep the filling packed into the tooth.

The preparation of a tooth to receive a composite does not require as much tooth structure be removed. This is because an etching material is used to roughen the surface of the tooth that will allow the material to be bonded to the tooth structure itself.

CROWNS

When a tooth is prepared for a crown, the enamel is drilled away. The amount removed depends on the thickness of the material used to make the crown. When the crown is cemented, the tooth will be the original size and shape as before the dental work was done.

The crown is a full coverage restoration. This means it covers the entire tooth that is exposed above the gumline. It is like a glove, custom made to fit with the adjacent teeth and to precisely mesh with the opposing teeth.

Remember there are down sides of completely covering a tooth with any material; this may inhibit the natural detoxing of the tooth.

Most crowns are made of metal and most of those contain nickel or palladium. Even the white crowns, made for cosmetic purposes, are typically made with a metal base and a tooth colored ceramic baked on top, to custom-match the shade of the neighboring teeth.

There are crowns that do not have these metal bases that seem to be healthier and easier to tolerate for most people. Cerec, Dicor, Empress, Cernate, Targis - Vectris are just a few of the better options for materials.

A crown should only be done as a last resort, when the tooth requires the support to function.

INLAYS AND ONLAYS

Inlays are similar in size to fillings, but are usually fabricated in labs like crowns. This makes them more durable than fillings. When there is a large area to restore, this will be a better option than a composite filling. Many dentists will not do inlays or onlays because it requires more time and skill on the part of the dentist to create. It is like trying to recreate a lost puzzle piece in a jigsaw puzzle. Not only do you have to create the masterpiece but it must return from the lab and fit with precision into the missing area of tooth. Because of the combination of longer time required in the chair for the procedure, higher skill required by the dentist and low reimbursement from insurance companies, most dentists choose to do the crowns instead of the inlays or onlays.

The onlay will cover a larger portion of the tooth than the inlay but both allow a portion of the original tooth to remain. This gives the tooth a window to excrete toxins and is much healthier than the full coverage crown.

Again, consideration must be made about the materials used to make the inlay or onlay.

IMPLANTS

A metal commonly used in dental implants is Titanium. Chemical-toxic reaction can occur as tissue is damaged due to metal ions, respectively metal hydroxides. Focus-toxic reactions will progress to general reactions since the white blood cells will increase and the phagocytosis border value will be exceeded on a local basis.[34] This is why some people's body's reject the implanted metal, thus causing the implant to fail.

To the various and diverse clinical symptoms, we must add the following side effects of metal implants: Subjective symptoms such as metallic taste, increased sensitivity to spices and foods, burning and tongue itching and neuralgic complaints. Localized symptoms such as blue-gray pigmented areas in the gum tissue, ulcerations, swollen gum tissue and leukoplakias (white plaque) of the mucosa. Regional symptoms may include eczema of the face. This is due to the skin making an effort to detox the metal. General symptoms may manifest themselves in headaches and increased nervous irritability.

Because titanium is a transition metal (one that gives away electrons and forms strong complexes with organic and inorganic ligands) placing it in a mouth with amalgams, will make the mercury and copper release at a faster pace causing the fillings to corrode faster.

Beyond the body's chemical toxic burden response, consideration must be given to the energetic response of an implanted metal.

What happens when you stick a metal 2 tonged fork into an electric wall socket? You create a short in the circuit. When metal is implanted into the body you can create a short on the entire energetic meridian.

In rare cases where there is not enough jaw bone left to fit a pair of dentures, implants may be an option to no teeth.

Top on your list would be having compatibility testing done to assure you will not react to the metal implants.

Be sure to have your implants cleaned at an office familiar with their care. You will damage an implant by using the conventional metal scalers that the hygienist uses. Special plastic scalers are used for cleaning the implants. People who have chosen to have implants need to protect that investment with perfect daily oral hygiene.

PARTIAL PLATE AND FULL DENTURES

Remember, when it becomes necessary to replace teeth with a partial or full denture, you really want to avoid any metal in your prosthesis (partial or denture). This is especially true if the appliance crosses from one side of your mouth to the other, going over the midline.

Examples: an upper partial that covers the roof of your mouth or a lower one that has metal going behind the lower front teeth.

No metal means, no metal wires; even for the clasps.

Ask about the coloring agent used to make the pink or red part. That pink simulates the gum tissue. Does it contain cadmium? Many of them do. Valplast is a nylon material that does not use any metals in the pink. Different materials are available to manufacture the desired prosthesis. Again, I stress that testing be done to insure the most biocompatible material is used.

REMOVEABLE IS BEST

Why have removable appliances to replace missing teeth? Conventional dentistry claims fixed crown and bridge restorative work as the Cadillac of dental work. Craniosacral work shows us that tying the teeth together, restricts the movement and alters the flow of energy. Ever floss your teeth and notice that some days they are tighter than other days? Your body has a natural ebb and flow of the sutures in the skull. I have seen patients improve the status of their health by removing fixed dental work and going to removable partials.

Why crown the teeth and risk smothering them? This is a crime to do especially if the two teeth did not need dental work and the work is just being done to replace the missing tooth.

"But I can't bare the thought of wearing, Granny Teeth". Change your attitude. They aren't "Granny Teeth". They are more like a retainer a youth would wear after orthodontic treatment. Having bridges placed is a burden. When you have enough good health to spare that you can afford to give some away, you could always consider bridgework. Go for the health first.

FIXED BRIDGES

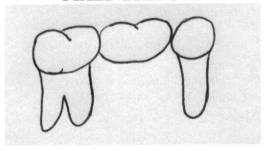

Three unit Fixed Bridge replacing a missing molar by crowning the teeth on either side

The thing that really bothers me about fixed bridge work is the need to do dental work on the adjacent teeth to hold the bridge. Making a bridge usually involves crowning the teeth on either side of the missing tooth. The teeth that hold the bridge are called abutment teeth. The crown that is suspended between the abutment teeth (the space of the extracted tooth) is called a pontic. If you do not remember the drawbacks to crowning a tooth, go back and reread that section. If those abutment teeth are not in need of crowns and you are doing dental work on them just for the sake of a lost tooth, then shame on you. THERE IS NO DENTAL MATERIAL COMPARABLE TO WHAT GOD GAVE YOU! Why risk damaging two other teeth. Get a removable partial.

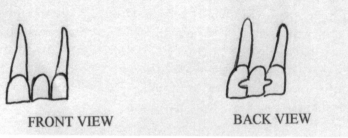

FRONT VIEW   BACK VIEW

Maryland Bridge replacing one front tooth without crowning the adjacent teeth

Another type of bridge is the Maryland bridge. This type of bridge has a crown as the pontic with wings extending out both sides of the crown. The teeth on either side are drilled to receive the wings and the bridge is bonded in place. At least with this style of bridge, the teeth on either side are not crowned.

Usually bridges are made out of metal, to handle the stress of the load. There are some new, non-metallic materials, which seem to be able to handle the pressure needed for fixed bridge work. Artglass and Targis-Vectris are two materials that show promise. These conservative bridges still pose the burden of connecting the teeth.

Conventional dentists will tell you that fixed bridge work is the best that dentistry has to offer. They will tell you that bridges will feel more natural than partials, (and that is true). There is quite a bit of profit in fixed bridges for the dentist. Replacing one tooth with a bridge means, the cost will be for three crowns soldered together. Replacing a space where two adjacent teeth are missing means, the bridge will consist of four crowns. The cost of crowns vary from $600- $1200 each. Simple math will mean a substantial investment on the part of the patient is about to occur. If decay reoccurs, the chances are very high that the bridge will be replaced with a new one. Caring for your investment will mean daily flossing to prevent decay on the abutment teeth under the bridge. At least try the removable one first. You can always go with the fixed bridge later if you wish.

Many craniosacral therapists believe it is not healthy or natural to tie teeth together. This prevents the natural ebb and flow the teeth have come to know. Bridging teeth ties them together. Restricting the movement can stress the tooth and the related meridian.

I was fortunate to meet and work with a woman from Germany. Her son does craniosacral work here in the USA. She had 6 front crowns that, when placed, were connected with solder like a bridge would be. Not only did this make cleaning between her teeth a more difficult task, but she started having health problems. At the advice of her son, she had the dentist disconnect the crowns. She was amazed with the results.

After that incident, a patient was referred to me because she started having severe trigeminal pain (facial pain) after a three unit bridge was placed by a dentist in the area. I requested the dentist remove the bridge and place temporary crowns on the abutment teeth. Her pain abated within a few days. Later, she tried a fixed bridge again and the pain returned. The bridge was removed and the pain ceased. Finally, she had permanent crowns placed on the abutment teeth and left the space so a removable partial could be placed.

If you notice problems after the bridge is in place, remember the craniosacral philosophy.

CHAPTER EIGHT

DENTAL TRAUMA

Teeth that receive trauma, respond in different ways. Some teeth handle the stress and stay healthy for a lifetime. Some teeth lose their vitality in the weeks that immediately follow the trauma. In other cases, a tooth may die years after the accident. In some cases, a debris- filled pulp chamber is left. Death may occur so slowly that essentially the body does its own root canal and the tissue inside the canals calcifies. Because the process is slow, the body carries off the toxins and handles the infection on an everyday basis until the clean-up is complete. Often times there are no abscess or fistula seen. Discoloration of the tooth or observation on x-ray may be the first sign on which to base a diagnosis. This area of degeneration creates an energy block to the tooth's corresponding meridian.[35]

This trauma-induced death could be from an accidental blow to a tooth or from orthodontic work (when a tooth is moved too quickly by the orthodontist   or reacts poorly to the moving process). When damage is due to some form of treatment it is termed an *iatrogenic* cause.

Another iatrogenic cause for tooth trauma is just now being hypothesized. Dr. Doug Cook DDS believes, using a high speed drill creates a vacuum during the drilling process. This vacuum sucks healthy tissue out of the tubules in the tooth. This allows bacteria to get inside the tubules that are now under the filling. The bacteria slowly manipulate their way into the nerve, releasing toxins and causing death to the tooth. In the past, the theory has been that the nerve could have been traumatized as it was subjected to the heat generated during the drilling process. Dr. Cook's philosophy suggests abandonment of the high speed drills and recommends returning the dentist to the slow speed drill, under 20,000 rpm.[36] This would eliminate both the heat and the vacuum effect.

Newer techniques using air abrasion or drill-less

dentistry, provide a promising future for the least amount of trauma induced while preparing the tooth. The air abrasion uses a powder to blow away the decay and modify the tooth to accept a restoration, with the least amount of damage to the rest of the tooth. The powder seals tubules as it goes and less heat generated means less of a need to anesthetize the tooth.

The use of the conventional drill causes small micro-fractures in the enamel. These micro-fractures weaken the tooth structure and may provide inlets for bacteria introduction. Imagine drilling a hole in a fine china plate with your drill at home. The high speed drills generate so much heat that a spray of water is used to help cool the tooth. Does the dentist you use have an individual filter on that water line? If not, as those tubules are being vacuumed they are being filled with impure water filled with bacteria.

MALOCCLUSION OR TMJ

Whenever two teeth hit prematurely, the body tries to kick in a protective mechanism, muscles in the head and neck make adjustments. These adjustments can cause headaches and spasms along with neck-aches. This is often experienced by a patient after recent dental work when a new filling or crown is placed. This can be corrected by adjusting the height of the new restoration, returning the teeth to a proper bite.

TMJ or Tempromandibular Joint Syndrome can be caused by poor alignment of the muscles, the jaws or the teeth. There are dentists that specialize in TMJ problems. The patients usually go through bite adjustments and wear splints to relax burdens on muscles or retrain the muscles to another bite. Some patients wear occlusal splints when they sleep to prevent grinding their teeth or clenching at night. Some bites are so sensitive that the patient will benefit from a chiropractic adjustment just before the dental appointment. Use of a TENS unit is becoming popular to help the jaw muscles relax and allow the joint to find its natural resting position.

There are three main reasons for TMJ dysfunction, 1) tooth loss 2) malocclusion 3) developmental abnormalities. *First*, is the loss of teeth, either through decay or trauma. If these missing teeth are not replaced, shifting of the remaining teeth tends to occur. Teeth will drift into an open space, not just sideways but up and down. A missing upper molar may cause the bottom tooth that it used to meet, to grow or extrude into the area where the missing tooth used to be. Now the taller bottom tooth has less of the root anchored in the lower jaw. This means that the root surface is now above the gum and is vulnerable to decay because there is no enamel on the root surface. With less of the tooth in solid bone the tooth is less stable. Chewing forces may rock the tooth causing it to loosen. Teeth are meant to withstand tremendous chewing forces in an up and down motion. If a tooth leans into an extraction site, the force will be similar to wiggling a tooth several hours a day. Finally, it will destroy the bone support and loosen. This is why it is so important to replace missing teeth or orthodontically move them into a good relationship.

The *Second* reason for TMJ dysfunction is the teeth's chewing surfaces are too high or too low. This is commonly seen after dental restorations, where a filling may make a tooth a little taller than it was before the treatment. This causes the tooth to hit harder and prematurely causing a bruise to the ligament. Ever had a stone bruise on your foot? Even if there is no rock in your shoe now it will take a while to heal. You step on your heel later and waves of pain shoot up your leg. Now imagine the rock is there for several weeks.

Without correction (by adjusting the height of the restoration) the tooth could suffer irreparable damage to the nerve and die. The same bruising can happen if, while chewing, you accidentally find a piece of gristle or a shell. Usually there is pain to the tooth for several days to a couple weeks as the bruise heals. This same trauma can happen to teeth that are clenched or ground on a regular basis. Some people will clench or grind teeth in their sleep in times of stress. This will need the attention of a dentist trained in making occlusal splints, to prevent contact of the teeth and leave the muscles of the head and neck in a neutral state. A sign that one is clenching at night may be tender neck muscles or the muscles above the ear going toward the forehead. Years of clenching may cause the cheek or buccinator muscles to enlarge. This gives the patients thicker cheeks due to continued exercise of those muscles. Some people may find that they clench or grind during the daytime. Use of the splints are also helpful during the day. The first step would be a, "Lips together, teeth apart" approach. Retraining oneself and making a conscious effort to stop the clenching is not an easy task, but it is possible.

The *Third* reason is developmental abnormalities of the maxilla (upper jaw) and the mandible (lower jaw). A link has been found with the increased intake of processed sugar and flour to the poor development of the jaw. Most people are familiar with the profile of the "buck tooth" or "bulldog" individual. The upper or lower jaw is disproportionate to the other. This may require surgery to shorten the jaw or expanders can be used on children to promote growth of a jaw.

The primary mechanism necessary for supplying nutrients to the body is chewing. If the jaws or teeth are not aligned properly, the entire cranium will distort in order to chew properly. This distortion stresses the body and can be responsible for headaches, low back pain, neck pain, insomnia, loss of concentration and depression.

If the bite is off it can shift the relationship of the 1st

two vertebrae, the Atlas and Axis. As the spinal cord comes out of the skull, compression of the cord will occur if they are not aligned properly. Pressure on the nerves that go to the elbow or as far away as the ankle may be pinched. Any pressure on the cord can cause problems anywhere in the body.

Diagnosis of dysfunction of the TMJ is made by a dentist trained in this area. He will make note of popping or clicking in the joint upon opening and closing, observe facial symmetry, midline shift of teeth upon opening, asymmetric wear on chewing surfaces of teeth, and tenderness of the joint. He may also use diagnostic tools like X-rays, MRI, Applied Kinesiology and Electrodermal screening (EAV).[37] X-rays may reveal excess wear on the joint itself or deformity to the joint caused from years of poor occlusion or fit of the teeth.

Treatment of TMJ may include:

1) Wearing an occlusal splint while sleeping and for some people, during waking hours.

2) Orthodontic treatment may be needed to improve the bite relationship.

3) Surgery may be indicated in some cases. In some severe cases, crowns may be placed on certain teeth to open a bite. This would be done if the joint was being damaged by all the teeth being too short. Years of grinding will shorten the teeth.

4) Chiropractic Adjustments may prove beneficial.

5) Massage therapy may be helpful.

6) Another form of treatment is Craniosacral therapy. Craniosacral therapy gently manipulates the bones of the skull to treat a range of conditions, from headache to overall body function.

CHAPTER NINE

CHELATING AND DETOXING

Heavy metal detoxification is a long process that can take six months to several years to accomplish. Often a DMPS (Dimercaptopropane sulfonate) challenge is done to document high levels of heavy metals. DMPS use forms complexes with heavy metals like mercury, cadmium, arsenic, lead, copper, silver, tin and others and is then excreted through the kidneys. EDTA (Ethylene Diamine Tetra Acetate) can be used to help remove the mercury. The most important rule to observe when using EDTA is to take the treatment slowly. The IV will run for two to three hours, per treatment. Multiple treatments will typically be needed. Nutritional supplementation is *essential for insuring health* during the chelation process. Chelating agents not only bind to the mercury, but they also bind with minerals normally found in our body, minerals we need to perform daily cellular functions. This makes taking vitamins and minerals to replace ones pulled out in the process of chelating, a necessity.

Realize that removing the heavy metals from cells may come in waves. You will get a release and then maybe a week, a month or even a few months later you may dump more from your cells. Some people feel fatigued for a few days following each release.

There are certain routes your body uses to remove rubbish and toxins. These routes are called **excretory routes**. The lymphatics scavenge the blood for toxins, the lungs try to exhale the toxins, the large intestines dump toxins out via the feces, the liver detoxifies everything we put into our body and the kidneys filter our urine. Sweat takes things out via the skin. These excretory routes help keep our bodies working in a toxic world.

Here in an analogy of how important cleaning these routes and getting them open and prepared for the work of chelating is. Go home and clean a room of your house. Now, gather everything into a garbage bag to throw out. When you try to throw it out you notice all the doors and windows are locked, prohibiting you from throwing the bag away. You did move things but you have not **removed** or discarded them. It is easy to mobilize toxins in the body and move them around but if those excretory routes are not open, you have not excreted them! An excellent protocol is called "Opening the Channels" by Energetics. Their website is www.goenergetix.com.

Before you get ready to get rid of those heavy metals you need to be sure you are drinking enough water. Drink at least half your body weight, in ounces of water daily. (e.g.: 150 lb person requires 75 oz. of water per day) If you are not drinking the required amount of water, the toxins get thicker and become more difficult to remove. Our body is created to function best when we give it water to clean the debris on a daily basis. Try not to drink your water at meals as this dilutes your digestive enzymes. Drinking no more than 4 oz. in a 15 minute interval will allow time for the tissues to absorb the water. Sipping water with a little lemon or lime is a great habit to get into. Your bowels should move easily at least once a day, EVERY day. You should learn to do limbic breathing exercises. Any Yoga class will teach limbic breathing. This is a style of breathing that expands your abdomen and allows more air volume into the lungs. Use herbals to stimulate cleaning of the liver tissues. Rebounding may be done by jumping on a small trampoline and is an excellent way to stimulate the lymphatics. For those that can not jump, the use of dry brushing the skin daily also stimulates the lymphatics. For this you will use a hair brush and go over the entire body before showering. This loosens dry and dead skin and stimulates the lymphatics.

Enzymes are a big help in all of this. They do so many things that I will just touch on a few. They assist in breaking up debris throughout the body and help digestion too. Because so many of these dental toxins from root canals and cavitation sites inhibit the body from being able to produce some of these vital enzymes needed to produce ATP, you feel fatigued. You will need good quality replacement. I suggest contacting Transformation Enzymes   800-777-1474. Their founder and president Dr. DicQie Fuller Looney has authored several books that go into detail, but make it easy to understand why you can't live without these lifesaving proteins.

Now that the doors and windows have been opened to throw out the trash, the next step is to make sure you will not be reactive to the toxins as they come out of the intracellular areas into the extracellular spaces. This is best done by a practitioner skilled in Allergy Elimination. N.A.E.T. (Nambudripad's Allergy Elimination Technique) is a technique designed to determine potential allergens and eliminate the body's desire to overreact. This technique was developed by Dr. Devi Nambudripad D.C., L.Ac., R.N., Ph.D. and is a totally noninvasive way to identify and eliminate allergens.

There are some incredible oral chelating agents now available. Extended Health has a formula created by Dr. Maile Poules Ph.D. It is taken twice daily and provides agents to bind to heavy metals and chemicals, but also replaces good minerals that are traditionally lost in the process of chelating. Clinical experience proves it's effectiveness at removing heavy metals and clearing coronary arteries of plaque. Their website is www.extendedhealth.com

Another wonderful agent is *Metal Free*. This is effective at binding to toxic metals that are harmful, and less to the good minerals. This creates less of a risk of mineral imbalances. This may be used on infants and children with incredible results. Their website is www.metalfree.com

CHAPTER TEN

ALLERGIES

There has been considerable time spent explaining the different metals and the toxic effects that some metals have. When it comes to dentistry and its materials, many can be reactive to the patient. There are cements, anesthetics, bonding materials, temporary materials, denture materials and more. Remember, there are options to finding compatible dental materials. There is a blood test, electrodermal screening and applied kinesiology. The blood test offers results that are true allergens. What about materials that aren't true allergens, they don't cause hyper-reactivity or anaphylaxis, yet they cause an energetic reaction with your body?[38]

Here is an example: Mr. Smith wears a new watch and, for some reason, when he wears the watch, it stops running. It will not keep time. Mr. Smith removes the watch and places it on his night stand and to his amazement the watch begins to tick. Here, we have a reaction that is visible, a substance entering our electromagnetic field with disharmony as a result. Mr. Smith's electromagnetic field seemed to make the watch react a certain way. Could the watch also have an effect on Mr. Smith? The answer is, yes. Is Mr. Smith allergic to the watch? No, this is an energetic reaction and in this case, the watch lost.

Some people come home and the first thing they do is remove their watch, necklace and rings. When asked why, they may respond, "I just feel better without them". This is an energetic reaction where the person is losing, energetically speaking.

Another example of reactivity vs. true allergy could be found in eating Chinese food, containing high amounts of MSG. For some individuals this may cause a headache. Every time they eat the MSG they get the same reaction, a headache. If they ask the chef to prepare the dish without the MSG, no headache. Now, if this person decided to go to a traditional allergist and was told that their tests were negative for an allergy to MSG, how would you explain the headache? Well, it may not be an allergy that creates antibodies but it certainly is a reaction none-the-less and an unwanted one.

The advantage to kinesiology and electrodermal testing is that the reactive materials showing up on the blood test are found, along with those that are energetically reactive. Those materials that cause energetic reactions do not show on blood tests. In the cases of the watch and the MSG, they would both show up as reactive items if using either Muscle testing or Electrodermal testing. Another disadvantage to the blood testing is having to go to a lab for a blood draw. Additionally, sending the results off may delay treatment by a couple of weeks. Another disadvantage is you will only show allergies for things you have been exposed to at least once in your life. Being exposed causes your body to create antibodies to the offending substance. It is difficult to determine an allergy to something by using blood if you have never been exposed to it. This means you could have some false negatives. A false negative means a material may test OK because you have never been exposed to it, but ends up not being a compatible material.

Placing a dental material in your mouth is a 24 hour a day exposure that you can't get away from. We don't want anything that causes either a true allergic reaction or even an energetic reaction.

Kinesiology will give only yes or no answers. The skilled practitioner will be able to identify materials that may cause reactions and be more selective than blood tests. Here we are able to test items that you have never been exposed to and by using your body's biofeedback abilities, one can get a feel for items that weaken the individual.

Electrodermal screening gives you a number guide, not just a yes or a no, but a *how yes* and a *how no*. This will allow the dentist to know more than just which materials are compatible, but which materials appear to be the absolute best for that patient. Like the muscle testing, you can determine reactions to things the person has never previously been exposed to.

Aren't there some materials that are compatible for everyone? No, I have not found **any** items that will work for **every** patient. There are certainly some materials that are better tolerated by more people than other materials. I have even had some people that have such weak immune systems, that they can't even handle some of the best tolerated materials until they boost their immune systems.

Is it possible to test reactive to something energetically and be able to handle it later? Yes, this is the case when the immune system is in absolute overload and just can't handle anything that is not what God gave us in the first place. These are the people that can't tolerate foods they once ate. As the immune system gets healthier, they can eat those foods again and they can tolerate some materials that they might not have been suited for at the time of testing.

Then is it possible to test tolerant to a material and not test well later? Of course, if your immune system spirals out of control you may become intolerant of those items.

Replacing known toxins like mercury, nickel and thallium for more compatible materials is a big deal. Dental materials are changing for the better every year.

Often the person with high mercury levels has high levels of Candida in their body. This high Candida level will tax the immune system and they seem to be reactive to things that have never been a problem for them in the past. As the person changes their diet, has fillings removed, goes through chelation and finally gets the Candida under control, their quote "allergies" improve.

While on the subject of materials causing energy imbalances, I would like to explain two metals; gold and silver. Gold acupuncture needles are used to stimulate. Silver needles are used to depress. Upon removal of old silver fillings, some people have an almost immediate surge of energy, while others seem to have a gradual increase, taking months to achieve the same improvement. I had this phenomenon explained to me by a doctor well versed in the subject.[39] The patients that had an immediate surge of energy, had been reacting to the silver in the filling material. Silver causes a depression of energy to the body. The ones that took longer to notice the energy return were reacting to the reduction of mercury level. These people improved as they chelated the mercury out of their bodies. He went on to explain that he had seen several people have extreme changes for the worse after having gold dental work placed. His opinion was the gold stimulated the disease process. Upon his recommendation these people had the gold removed and their health improved. Remember, dental gold has other metals mixed in for strength, adding to the possibility of energy problems and electro galvanic reactions. I have witnessed people with high blood pressure have their gold fillings and crowns replaced, and their blood pressure return to normal. This has happened more often when the teeth involved were the lower molars, as they are on the artery and vein meridian.

CHAPTER ELEVEN

TOOTH / BODY CONNECTION

Can A Problem in an Organ be Related to a Tooth?

Remember what a meridian is? It is a term that identifies a pathway or channel that "Chi" (energy) flows on. This is like invisible wiring that carries energy.

The easiest way to see the meridians with the organs and teeth is to list the teeth one at a time. You may use the chart on page 107 by finding the appropriate tooth and following the blocks vertically, or you may locate the organ and it will lead you to a tooth. As you look through the chart you will notice the maxillary molars and mandibular bicuspids cross the same meridians. Find a cuspid on the chart and look in the area marked sense organ. Did you ever hear of a cuspid being called an eye tooth? That name was not given without a good reason.

Look at the chart on the next pages. See tooth #1? That is the upper right third molar. Find #15. That is the upper left second molar, also called the twelve year molar. Find #19. That is the lower left first molar, also called the six year molar. Finally, find #29. That is the lower right second bicuspid. Don't worry, with practice it will be easy.

Every tooth has a meridian going to it. There are 12 meridians and each of the 32 teeth are represented on those meridians. The bicuspids share a meridian, the molars share another meridian and the anterior (front) teeth share a common meridian. The maxillary bicuspids share with the mandibular molars and the maxillary molars share with the mandibular bicuspids.

Remember, the meridians can be effected anywhere along the path. A maxillary six year molar with a root canal could be the cause of a stomach problem, or the stomach problem could be affecting the six year molar. It is important to get an analysis from a qualified practitioner to confirm where the block is occurring. Think of the meridian as a giant

105

freeway, making a circle around a city. There are several exit and entrance ramps placed on this freeway. These ramps allow energy to flow from the meridian, to the organ and from the organ back to the meridian. Imagine knowing it should take an hour to complete one circle on this imaginary freeway but today it seems slow. Then imagine sending a helicopter to locate the traffic blockage and report where the blockage is. With this information you can make choices about what to do. This imaginary scenario is what happens when you use electrodermal screening or what is also called Meridian Stress Assessment to identify flow of energy and blockages on the meridian pathways.

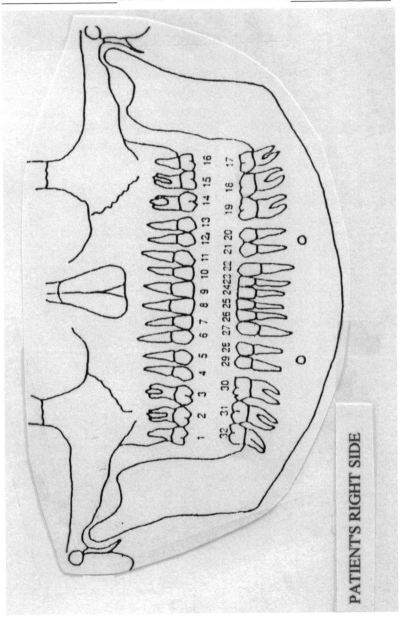

PATIENT'S RIGHT SIDE

Tooth#1- Upper right third molar (wisdom tooth)- Anterior lobe of the Pituitary gland, internal ear on right side, part of the tongue on the right, ulnar side of right shoulder, Plantar side of right foot, right toes, ulnar side of right elbow, ulnar side of right hand, sacro-iliac joint on right, segments of spinal marrow and dermatomes (SC1, SC2, SC8, STH1, STH5, STH6, STH7, SS1, SS2), Vertebrae (C1, C2, C7, TH1, TH5, TH6, TH7, S1, S2), right side of the heart, duodenum, terminal ileum on the right, central nervous system, limbic system The mid Trapezius muscle.

Tooth#2- Upper right second molar- shares with #3. *The right side of Parathyroid gland and the right side of abdominal muscle relate to #2 only.*

Tooth #3- Upper right first molar -Tongue on right, maxillary sinus, oropharynx, larynx, jaw on right side, right anterior hip, right anterior knee, right medial ankle joint, spinal marrow and dermatomes (SC1, SC2, STH11, STH12, SL1), vertebrae (C1, C2, TH11, TH12, L1), Pancreas, Esophagus, right side of stomach, right breast. *The right latissimus dorsi and the right side of Thyroid relate to #3 only.*

Tooth #4- Upper right second bicuspid- shares with #5. *The Thymus gland, right breast and the right side of diaphragm muscle relate to tooth #4 only.*

Tooth #5- Upper right first bicuspid- Nose on right side, ethmoid sinus, radial side of shoulder on the right, radial side of elbow on the right, radial side of hand on the right, right foot, big toe on right foot, spinal marrow and dermatomes (SC1, SC2, SC5, SC6, SC7, STH2, STH3, STH4, SL4, SL5), vertebrae (C1, C2, C5, C6, C7, TH2, TH3, TH4, L4, L5), right lung, bronchi, large intestine on right side. The pectoralis major clavicular relates to both tooth #4 and #5. *The right coracobrachialis popliteus and Posterior lobe of pituitary gland relate to #5 only.*

Tooth#6- Upper right cuspid- Intermediate lobe of the Pituitary gland, Hypothalamus, posterior portion of the right eye, sphenoidal sinus, tonsilla palate, posterior portion of right knee, right hip, lateral side of right ankle, spinal marrow and dermatomes (SC1, SC2, STH8, STH9, STH10), vertebrae (C1, C2, TH8, TH9, TH10), right side of liver, gall bladder, biliary ducts on the right side. The right deltoid and right anterior serratus.

Tooth #7 Upper right lateral incisor- same meridian as #8. *The right subscapularis relates to tooth #7 only.*

Tooth #8 Upper right central incisor- Pineal gland, the nose, sphenoidal sinus and frontal sinus on the right side, posterior right knee, right sacro-coccygeal joint, posterior right ankle joint, spinal marrow and dermatomes (SC1, SC2, SL2, SL3, SS3, SS4, SS5, SCo) vertebrae (C1, C2, L2, L3, S3, S4, S5, SCo), right kidney, right side of bladder, ovary, testicle, prostate, uterus, rectum, anal canal. *The right side neck flexors and extensors relate to #8 only.*

Tooth#9 Upper left central incisor- Pineal gland, the nose, sphenoidal sinus and frontal sinus on the left side, posterior left knee, left sacro-coccygeal joint, posterior left ankle joint, spinal marrow and dermatomes (SC1, SC2, SL2, SL3, SS3, SS4, SS5, SCo), vertebrae (C1, C2, L2, L3, S3, S4, S5, SCo), left kidney, urinary bladder left side, ovary, testicle, prostate, uterus, rectum, anal canal. *The left side neck flexors and extensors relate to tooth #9.*

Tooth #10 Upper left lateral incisor- same as #9. *The left subscapularis relates to #10 only.*

Tooth #11 Upper left cuspid- Intermediate lobe of pituitary gland, hypothalamus, posterior portion of the left eye, sphenoidal sinus on the left, tonsilla palate, posterior of left knee, left hip, lateral side of left ankle, spinal marrow and dermatomes (SC1, SC2, STH8, STH9, STH10), vertebrae (C1, C2, TH8, TH9, TH10), left side of liver, bilary ducts left side. The left deltoid and left anterior serratus.

Tooth #12 Upper left first bicuspid- Left side of nose, ethmoidal cells, radial side of left shoulder, radial side of left elbow, radial side of left hand, left foot, big toe on left foot, spinal marrow and dermatomes (SC1, SC2, SC5, SC6, SC7, STH2, STH3, STH4, SL4, SL5), vertebrae, (C1, C2, C5, C6, C7, TH2, TH3, TH4, L4, L5), left lung, bronchi, large intestine on the left side. The pectoralis major clavicular relates to #12 and #13. *The left coracobrachialis popliteus and posterior lobe of pituitary gland relates to #12 only.*

Tooth #13 Upper left second bicuspid- Shares the meridian with #12. *The Thymus gland, breast and the left diaphragm relate to #13 only.*

Tooth #14 Upper left first molar- *Thyroid gland relates to #14 only.* Tongue on the left, maxillary sinus, orapharynx, larynx, left side of jaw, anterior left hip, anterior left knee, left medial ankle joint, spinal marrow and dermatomes (SC1, SC2, STH11, STH12, SL1), vertebrae (C1, C2, TH11, TH12, L1), Spleen, Esophagus, left side stomach, left breast. *Tooth #14 is related to the left latissimus dorsi.*

Tooth #15 Upper left second molar- Shares meridian with #14. *The Parathyroid gland and the left abdominal muscle relate to #15 only.*

Tooth#16 Upper left third molar (wisdom tooth)- Anterior lobe of Pituitary gland, internal ear on left side, part of tongue on the left side, ulnar side of left shoulder, Plantar side of left foot, left toes, ulnar side of left elbow, ulnar side of left hand, sacro-iliac joint on left, spinal marrow and dermatomes (SC1, SC2, SC8, STH1, STH5, STH6, STH7, SS1, SS2) vertebrae (C1, C2, C7, TH1, TH5, TH6, TH7, S1, S2), left side of heart, duodenum, ileum, jejunum, central nervous system, limbic system, mid trapezius muscle.

Tooth #17 Lower left third molar (wisdom tooth)- Tongue, Middle external ear, Sacro-iliac joint on left side, ulnar side of left hand, plantar side of left foot, toes, left shoulder, left elbow, spinal marrow and dermatomes (SC1, SC2, SC8, STH1, STH5, STH6, STH7, SS1, SS2), vertebrae (C1, C2, C7, TH1, TH5, TH6, TH7, S1, S2), left side of heart, left side of jejunum, left side of ileum, peripheral nerves, energy exchange, psoas muscle.

Tooth #18 Lower left second molar- shares the meridian with #19. *The arteries and the left quadriceps relate to tooth 18 only.*

Tooth #19 Lower left first molar- nose, ethmoid cells, radial side of left hand, foot, big toe, left shoulder, left elbow, spinal marrow and dermatomes (SC1, SC2, SC5, SC6, SC7, STH2, STH3, STH4, SL4, SL5), vertebrae (C1, C2, C5, C6, C7, TH2, TH3, TH4, L4, L5), left lung, left side of large intestine. *The veins and the left muscles gracilis and sartorius relate to #19 only.*

Tooth #20 Lower left second bicuspid- shares the meridian with #21. *The lymph vessels, and the left pect. maj. sternal relate to tooth 20 only.*

Tooth #21 Lower left first bicuspid- Tongue, left maxillary sinus, left jaw, left medial ankle joint, left anterior hip, left anterior knee, spinal marrow and dermatomes (SC1, SC2, STH11, STH12, SL1), vertebrae (C1, C2, TH11, TH12, L1), spleen, esophagus, stomach on left side, left mammary glands, hamstrings. *The left gonads and left quadratus lumborum relate to 21 only.*

Tooth #22 Lower left cuspid- Gonads, anterior portion of left eye, sphenoidal sinus, lateral left ankle joint, left hip, posterior left knee, spinal marrow and dermatomes (SC1, SC2, STH8, STH9, STH10), vertebrae (C1, C2, TH8, TH9, TH10), left side of liver, left biliary ducts, gluteus maximus.

Tooth #23 Lower left lateral incisor- shares the meridan with #24. *The left tensor fasciae latae and left pyriformis are related to #23 only.*

Tooth #24 Lower left central incisor- Adrenal gland, sphenoidal sinus, frontal sinus, posterior of left ankle joint, left sacro-coccygeal joint, posterior of left knee, spinal marrow and dermatomes (SC1, SC2, SL2, SL3, SS3, SS4, SS5, SCo), vertebrae (C1, C2, L2, L3, S3, S4, S5, Co)) Left kidney, rectum, anal canal, urinary bladder, left ovary/testicle, prostate/uterus. *The gluteus medius on the left side relates to #24 only.*

Tooth #25 Lower right central incisor- Shares meridian with #26. *The gluteus medius on the right side relates to #25 only.*

Tooth #26 Lower right lateral incisor- Adrenal gland, sphenoidal sinus, frontal sinus, posterior of right ankle, right sacro-coccygeal joint, posterior of right knee, Spinal marrow and dermatomes (SC1, SC2, SL2, SL3, SS4, SS5, SCo), vertebrae (C1, C2, L2, L3, S3, S4, S5, Co), Right kidney, rectum, anal canal, urinary bladder, right ovary/testicle, prostate/uterus. *The right Tensor Fasciae Latae and right Pyriformis relate to #26 only.*

Tooth #27 Lower right cuspid- Gonads, anterior portion of the right eye, sphenoidal sinus, lateral of right ankle joint, right hip, posterior of right knee, spinal marrow and dermatomes (SC1, SC2, STH8, STH9, STH10), vertebrae (C1, C2, TH8, TH9, TH10), right side of liver, biliary ducts right side, gallbladder, right gluteus maximus.

Tooth #28 Lower right first bicuspid- Shares the meridian with #29. *The right Gonads and right quadratus lumborum relate to 28 only.*

Tooth #29 Lower right second bicuspid- Tongue, right maxillary sinus, right jaw, medial of right ankle, right anterior hip, anterior of right knee, spinal marrow and dermatomes (SC1, SC2, STH11, STH12, SL1), vertebrae (C1, C2,TH11, TH12, L1), pancreas, esophagus, right side of stomach, right mammary glands, hamstrings. *The lymph vessels and the right pect. maj. sternal relate to 29 only.*

Tooth #30 Lower right first molar- Shares the meridian with #31. *The veins and the right muscles gracilis and sartorius relate to #30 only.*

Tooth #31 Lower right second molar- Nose, ethmoidal cells, radial side of right hand, right foot, big toe, right shoulder, right elbow, spinal marrow and dermatomes (SC1, SC2, SC5, SC6, SC7, STH2, STH3, STH4, SL4, SL5), vertebrae (C1, C2, C5, C6, C7, TH2, TH3, TH4. L4, L5), lung on right side, large intestine on right side, ileo-cecal area. *The arteries and the right quadriceps relate to #31 only.*

Tooth #32 Lower right third molar- (wisdom tooth) Tongue, middle external ear, sacro-iliac joint on right side, ulnar side of right hand, plantar side of right foot, toes, right shoulder, right elbow, spinal marrow and dermatomes (SC1, SC2, SC8, STH1, STH5, STH6, STH7, SS1, SS2), vertebrae (C1, C2, C7, TH1, TH5, TH6, TH7, S1, S2), right side of heart, terminal ileum, peripheral nerves, energy exchange, psoas muscle.

CHAPTER TWELVE

PERIODONTAL DISEASE

Periodontal disease is a disease of the bone and gums surrounding the teeth. The bone resorbs leaving little to support the teeth and they get loose. Statistics claim as high as 70% of adults have some form of periodontal disease.

Traditional dentists are very sure that brushing and flossing are the keys to maintaining healthy gum and bone tissue. The biological dentist will be looking at the whole person.

Sam Queen M.A. puts on an excellent course for dentists called "A Mouthful of Evidence." He explains to dentists and hygienists that periodontal disease is not confined to the mouth. We are starting to see mainstream medicine agree. The newest research shows periodontal patients are more likely to have cardiovascular problems. Who takes more x-rays on you than any doctor you go to? The answer is the dentist. So if changes are seen in bone density on your decay x-rays, he or she should refer you to a physician for a bone scan to check for osteoporosis.

The biological dentist or hygienist may take microscopic slides of the bacteria in your mouth and decide if the bacterium is normal or harmful. Periodontal patients often times have parasites or amoebas. Cutting the gums will not rid them of this problem. Sometimes getting rid of the bad organisms prevents surgery. Does the patient have a spouse that is infected? You don't want to have a source of re-infection. Does the patient use good hygiene techniques? This includes washing hands after use of the restroom and washing their fruits and vegetables. Do they wash eating utensils in very hot water to prevent cross contamination? I find grapefruit seed extract works wonders in certain situations. Other times what I see calls for tea tree oil. *Tooth and Gum* is a wonderful product available through a biological dentist. It is a non alcohol based mouthwash with essential oils and echinacea. The alcohol in mouthwashes will dry out the oral tissues and actually promote bad bacteria growth. There are several non-alcohol based mouthwashes on the market; read the labels.

Yes, brushing and flossing is still important, but the key? I am not so sure. There is an electric toothbrush out on the market called "Sonicare" that is an incredible tool. The frequency kills bacteria and the vibration passes through the gum tissue to help remove debris from the pockets. This in itself could prevent surgery with proper use.

Let's talk about brushing for just a minute. I am always asked what kind of toothpaste is best. NO TOOTHPASTE! That's right. If toothpaste really worked to remove plaque, then why not smear it between teeth before flossing? It is the mechanical action of the toothbrush bristles that remove the plaque, not the paste. Just as it is the mechanical action of the floss rubbing up and down that removes plaque from in-between the teeth. When you put toothpaste in your mouth, the taste deadens the taste buds on your tongue for about 10-20 minutes. Now that you have lost the tactile ability of your tongue, you cannot tell when your teeth are clean. Later as you are driving to work you feel a fuzzy spot on a tooth. That is a spot you missed but now you don't have a brush. Over days, the minerals in your saliva will cause that plaque to harden, like a hard water spot on your shower door, and this is now called tartar. If you will use the toothbrush with nothing on it, you will be able to feel when all the teeth are slick. Now they are clean! If you want to use toothpaste now, for the taste, you may. Please no pastes with fluoride. If you want to use a mouthwash, use one with no alcohol.

OK, I know you want to know about the fluoride. Years ago studies were done and results presented that have now been proven wrong. Fluoride can make bones weaker and areas with high fluoride concentrations have high cancer rates. If you want to know more, read "Fluoride the Aging Factor" by Dr. John Yiamouyiannis.

The gum tissue is connective tissue. Having a problem with the gums could mean you have a problem with all your connective tissue. This is an opportunity for nutritional counseling. CoQ10 is an enzyme normally found in the healthy body. Periodontal patients are found to be deficient in this enzyme. This is also a contributing factor in heart problems. Japan has been doing research with supplementing 30-100 mg of CoQ10 per day. The B vitamins are also important. Under stress they go out of the body so fast. Vitamin C helps build healthy collagen tissue. Your gums are made of collagen. Copper deficiencies can cause gum problems and decay.

I agree with mainstream dentistry's concept that tartar is like a splinter on the tooth. The body sees it as a foreign object and goes into an inflammatory state. This means white blood cells are sent to the area to try to destroy the foreign object. This is seen in the mouth as pus in a severe infection.

The biological dentist will know that when the patient is too acidic, phosphorus will leach from the bones. It does this in an effort to balance the pH. Staying in an acidic state, the body will die. When the phosphorus comes out of the bone, the calcium, now called free calcium falls out of the bone as well. In the mouth this is seen as bone loss or periodontal disease. The free calcium will deposit on the teeth and on the walls of arteries. Again we have a link of periodontal patients and cardiovascular problems. Part of the solution is teaching the patient to monitor their salivary pH and their urinary pH. A neutral pH is 7.0. Less than 7.0 is considered acidic and higher than 7.0 is consider alkaline.

First morning urine should be around 6.0-6.4 pH, if it is less than 6.0 the person is considered acidic. If the salivary pH is over 7.0 they will not be able to produce ptyalin in their saliva. This will prevent them digesting any carbohydrates (rice, pasta, bread, starches or fruits) that they may consume. This digestion problem will make them more acidic.

The acidic patient can be instructed about which foods are considered acid forming and can limit intake of those. An example would be sodas. They contain phosphoric acid which makes the body highly acidic. Drinking one soda would require about 10 glasses of water to neutralize the pH. This includes diet sodas. They should also be taught which foods are more alkalizing to the system and increase their intake.

As if all this weren't enough, imbalances in thyroid or adrenals can cause bone loss. Vitamin C levels may be too low. There are some simple tests to help rule this out and a biological dentist can provide you with information or direct you to an appropriate healthcare provider.

So, if you are about to undergo periodontal surgery, try to find the cause. If not, you may be in for a rude awakening and much frustration in trying to fight a losing battle.

CHAPTER THIRTEEN

BIOENERGETIC TESTING

Bioenergetic devices measure a direct or indirect biological response to an evoked potential, which is the response of the body to energy or a change in energy. The response allows the muscles to move, food to be digested, eyes to see, ears to hear and skin to feel. All functions use energy. Every process begins with energy.

The June 1996 issue of the Institute of Engineers magazine had several articles on acupuncture and the clinical aspects of Electro Acupuncture according to Voll (EAV). These abstracts confirmed the technology works.

EAV, Electrodermal screening, (EDS) also known as Meridian Stress Assessment (MSA) is an excellent tool for measuring the energy on the meridian. The principles of EDS are 1) use of Voll and acupuncture points 2) use of an ohmmeter to measure conductivity of electricity at those points.

Are there contraindications to using EDS? Yes, if the patient has a pacemaker it is discouraged. Even though it is not a problem for newer pacemakers, it is strongly advised against.

Using (EDS), the practitioner can measure different points along the path of the meridian to find the area where the conductance is poor. The patient holds on to a brass bar while the practitioner uses a brass probe held on an acupuncture point (usually on the hand or foot). This completes the circuit and a measurement of the electricity through the body can be obtained. The tooth can be stressed by gentle tapping or clenching and the reading taken again, using the same point. Because it is not invasive, this method is well tolerated by the patient.

Another method may be the use of applied kinesiology. In applied kinesiology, the muscle-gland-organ link can indicate the cause of the health problem and lead to further diagnostic tests for confirmation. Begin with a strong reading.

Then by touching the area, a weak muscle will indicate a problem. Having the patient hold a vial of the matching disease or toxin will again cause a change in the muscle strength, which is a match. It is important to stress the use of a properly trained, qualified, professional health care provider for tests such as these.

The dental anesthetic block is another tool available to determine the foci of the energy blockage. If the tooth is the cause of the pain (an example would be the knee), then the anesthetic will have a noticeable improvement for the patient. If there is no improvement, we assume the foci or cause is elsewhere.

Conventional dentistry has a testing device called a pulp tester. The principle is, if a small shock can be detected by the patient as the tooth is touched with a charged probe, then there must still be life. The idea is that a dead tooth has no nerve supply rendering it incapable of sending pain impulses. This device is not as sensitive to subtle changes in the health of the tooth as the alternative methods are.

DENTAL ASPECTS
OF
ELECTRO DERMAL SCREENING

Remember, EDS is a tool. If you take a temperature and it is high, does that mean you have an infection? If the temperature is too low, are you sick? I was surprised to learn while working my first marathon that some of the racers were hypothermic after the race. That means their body temperature was too low. Tools are used to help a doctor make a diagnosis. The doctor, not the tool makes the diagnosis. Does a high temperature mean you are having a heat stroke or that you have meningitis? The thermometer was a tool and the information the tool gave will be used by the doctor along with other information for the diagnosis to occur.

Now that we are clear about what the tool can and can not do, let's find out how it can be used to test teeth.

The object of the test is to identify what are called dental foci. A dental foci is an area of concentrated toxins that the body has attempted to wall off by surrounding the area with lymphocytes. This blocks the flow of energy on that pathway. The energy gets to the area, hits a black hole and disperses.

Illustration of Energy attempting to pass a Focal Disturbance

Testing the patient to assure they are in harmony with the earth's magnetic fields is called checking the spin. This must be done to assure accurate information.

There is a great measurement to use called a hand to hand measurement. This identifies a head foci. Holding a plain brass bar in one hand and the brass bar lead which is connected to the computer with the other, touch your probe to the plain bar. The normal reading should be 82-86. If the reading is over 86 there should be a foci located above the neck.

A healthy tooth or site in the mouth will measure between 45-55; just like any other measurement. The patient will hold the brass bar in the opposite side of the side you are trying to test. So, if you are testing teeth in the upper or lower right side, the patient will be holding the bar in the left hand.

Some practitioners are very intuitive and may test the teeth with just the graphic on the screen, progressing the screen, tooth by tooth.

Another way involves asking the patient to isolate the area with their finger, using the index finger of the hand holding the brass bar. This means the patient will be crossing the midline of their body to touch the area. As you progress on the screen tooth by tooth, the patient will touch the correct tooth that corresponds to the chart. Example: Tooth #1 (the upper right wisdom tooth) is on the screen, the patient holds the bar in the left hand. Their index finger on the left hand is inserted into the mouth and they touch the wisdom tooth or the gum where that tooth used to be.

A third way to test, is for the practitioner to stress the tooth or area, then test it. The stressing can be done by **1)** tapping the tooth with an instrument, **2)** by having the person bite on a wooden stick directly on the chewing surface applying moderate force or **3)** by electrically stimulating the area and then testing it.

When a tooth or area has a low or a high reading you would then look for the item that balances it. Watch for those falls or indicator drops! As we go through the different dental problems, you will get some ideas of things to look for.

CAVITATIONS

If you are testing an area where a tooth has been removed, have the patient isolate the area with the finger (or use one of the other methods). If the area has a low reading, this suggests a chronic long standing problem. The point you use is versatile. I choose to use the Ly2 point for mandibular teeth and the Ly3 point for the maxillary teeth. You can use the Ly2 for all the teeth if you choose. Another point that seems to get used a bit is the OR CMP. There are several things you could check. Here are some suggestions: Kieferostitis, Nosode Kieferostitis, Jaw Ostitis, Heavy Metals, Parasites, Lymes Disease, Botulinum. Let me explain what I do to balance a point. If the reading starts at 32 and Kieferostitis brings the reading closer to 50 but not exactly, place the Kiefer in the hold tank and output Kiefer two times (the one in the hold and the one in the output). If the reading comes still closer to 50 but still does not read 50, continue to repeat the step. Each of these outputs is representative of one ampule of the nosode. This is a way to quantify the intensity of the problem. If the point balances with one Kieferostitis, you may be successful at treating the area homeopathically. If it takes two outputs of the Kiefer to bring it to 50, it may be difficult to treat without surgery and require a longer treatment with herbs and homeopathics. Three amps of Kieferostitis will probably only be cleared with surgery. Four amps of Kieferostitis will surely require surgery.

If you get an elevated reading there may be an acute infection. Often, high levels of heavy metals or chemicals in the organs of that meridian will increase the rate and conductivity of electricity.

If you have an indicator drop, this suggests a diseased

area. Because our body is electrical it needs electricity to survive. If a certain amount of electricity goes in and as the measurement is taken the reading declines, there may be degenerative issues. Sick cells will steal the electricity as you are taking your reading. This shows up as a momentary reading of x with an end reading of y, with y being less than x. Example: the reading started out at 45, ended up at 39, leaving an indicator drop of of 6.

Be sure and check the areas behind the wisdom teeth. These are called the retromolar areas. They tend to be dump sites for all kinds of toxins.

I use the EDS during the surgery itself. At the beginning of the surgery, prior to the local anesthetic being administered, I take readings. I use the Ly CMP, Ly2, Ly3, Lu CMP, LI CMP, NE CMP, Cir CMP, AL CMP, OR CMP, TH CMP, HT CMP, SI CMP. Then I also test the area or site where the surgery is going to be done. If, for example, the surgery is being done where tooth #1 was removed years ago, I test the points I listed on the right hand only. Then using Ly3, I test the site of tooth #1. As the surgery progresses and the surgeon is removing the necrotic bone, this is what I experience. The points will clear in an order of best to worst, with the lowest reading being the last to clear. This shows me that the cavitation had an effect on all those meridians. When this happens the term Pan focus is used. This means the area involved effected more than just the meridian associated with it, the entire body was effected energetically. When the dentist wants to know if the site is clear, do the following. Have the dentist touch the socket with an instrument and try taking a reading. If it does not easily go to 50, have the dentist touch the mesial (toward the nose) of the socket. Take the reading again, do this on the distal (toward the ear) of the socket, the palatal, and the buccal. Any reading that is low will indicate the need to continue to clean the site further. It is my experience that the reading will go from the low original reading to a momentary high reading. This follows Herrings Law and makes perfect sense. There is another interesting finding in the surgery of cavitations. Sometimes the site takes time to clear, going from 35 up to 45 but not getting to 50. When the reading of 50 will repeat over and over, you can comfortably close the site. Many people that have observed surgery in our office are quite astonished with the procedure we have in place. What seems to amaze most people is that during surgery our computer is not within my field of vision. This means the readings are not influenced by me, they just are what they are, and we don't stop until they are 50, not 49 and not 51. This just shows how accurate the technique can be.

HOMEOPATHY BEFORE AND AFTER
THE SURGERY

I use lymph drainage with arnica and aconite at different chords. This should be started about three days prior to surgery if possible. The post surgery remedy is lymph drainage with several things chorded. I then take some of the proceeds from the surgery site (i.e. the root canal tooth or part of the bone and tissue from the site) and energetically put them in the lymph drainage, creating a customized remedy. This remedy has replaced most of our patients needs for conventional pain medications. By using the proceeds, you are making a homeopathic remedy called an autosode. In homeopathy, "like cures like". There is nothing more like than the actual substance. This way, without having to identify all the bacteria, you can customize a remedy for the patient.

The patient is given directions to take 10 drops every 15 minutes when awake for the first 2 days then at least 3 times a day there after. They are also told that they may use it as often as needed, without fear of overdosing. The usual conversation about care of a homeopathic remedy also takes place. Do not put it in your purse if you have a cell phone. Do not place it near anything that plugs in or has a battery.

COMPATIBILITY

The explanation I give patients when I am testing them against products that are in the system, is one that most people can understand. Imagine you are having an EEG run, measuring your brain wave activity. This is a way of measuring Biofeedback. Now, I expose you to a vibrational frequency (heavy metal rock music) and monitor the changes in the response. I then change the vibration to harp music, rap music, country music and so on. Your body will respond differently to those exposures of vibrational patterns.

Every substance known to man has its own unique frequency or vibrational pattern. I can measure the body's response to that vibrational pattern. These are energetic reactions not IgG or IgE reactions. There are over 700 different materials that could be used in dentistry. We can weed out 90% of those by looking at the chemical make up of the products. You really have to keep up with the new materials. Not all are good, but dental materials are ever changing and improving.

If 10 composite materials were checked and all were a yes with AK, with EDS we can know which yes is the best energetically. If eight of those items came out 54 one was 47 and one 50, we would select the item that measured a 50.

You need to know a little about homeopathy and the values of the potency. 1x is the closest to a mother tincture. This means it has the most molecules per cc. or mg. of substance. You will need to be sure to have your 1x (stress test) in the potency box turned on during testing of compatibility.

I choose to use the Allergy CMP for testing. I will also use the NE CMP or the OR CMP if I have a very sick person. The Allergy meridian crosses more surface area on your body so it is a great point. The nerve point may be used for MS patients or ones where the nerves are a key issue. The Organ point can also be good as a cross reference. Try testing off two points on those sensitive people.

It would be ideal if the base reading on the point was 50. That is not a key problem. If the base reading is 60, use that. Now if a substance takes you greater than five above or below that, it is not a match. If you have the time, you could balance the point to 50 and then test. The same holds true, above or below by five points is a mismatch for compatibility. I suggest you record the readings as you take them. Print the list and highlight the readings that deviate more than the five points. These would be materials that are not compatible.

If you do not have the product in the computer, place the sample on the tray. Be sure to set your system to 1x or stress. You should have an empty output box at this time. This way you are only testing the item on the tray.

Remember when balancing a point you are looking for items that bring your reading as close to 50 as possible. With allergy or compatibility testing, you want to note the items that took the base more than five away or had an indicator drop.

CHAPTER FOURTEEN

HOMEOPATHY

Homeopathy, frequently known as energy medicine, often deals with dilute concentrations of substances sometimes so dilute that there are no actual molecules of the original substance left, only the energy of it. To a person unfamiliar with the use of energy in healing, I offer the following example. If I had a unique set of foot prints, one foot with two toes and the other with three, and I walked barefoot on the beach, even after my physical being was gone you would know that I had been there. I left a distinct imprint in the sand with my unique footprints. Now, if you knew those footprints belonged to a serial killer, your reaction may be one of fear, just knowing that I had been there. Every substance known to man has a unique vibrational frequency or footprint. A second example goes as follows. My husband and I walk into a restaurant with another couple. As we enter, we hear our favorite song being played. We squeeze each other's hand and give each other a wink, as it elicits a response of warm fuzzies for the two of us. The couple that we entered with is clueless that the music is even being played. They do not respond like us, but they are not harmed or negatively effected.

There are certain laws in homeopathy that are worth mentioning. One is the "Law of Similars". This means, "like cures like". If you got stung by a bee and started to experience swelling, a homeopathic dose of Apis would bring the desired reaction of reduced swelling. Apis is the venom of a bee in dilute concentrations. If you wanted to induce vomiting, a vial of Syrup of Ipecac would be standard treatment. If while experiencing nausea and vomiting you wanted to use a homeopathic treatment, a homeopathic dose of Ipecac would bring the desired result. We are looking for substances that will resonate with the body and elicit a specific desired result. An example of an exact match of frequencies bringing a desired result, is when an opera singer hits that exact note that shatters the glass.

There are several great things to use for dental work.

Kava Kava- to calm down prior to an appointment.

Rescue Remedy or Five Flower Remedy- These are Bach flower remedies, good for calming.

Arnica- For trauma of pulling on cheeks, especially good when keeping mouth open for long periods.

Traumeel- Good to put on cheek after surgery.

Aconite- Good for fear, 12C or 30x, 5 pellets at night before bed and 5 before appointment.

Hypericum - For nerve pain in tooth. 30C- 3-5 pellets every 30 minutes until symptoms subside.

X-ray Homeopathic -30C Good after exposure to x-ray.

Homeopathics are best used if you refrain from eating or drinking 30 minutes before or after their use. If using pellets, do not touch the pellets. Shake them into a container and pour into mouth, allow to dissolve under tongue. Remedies should not be placed next to anything that has a battery or plugs in, as this alters their energy.

CHAPTER FIFTEEN

CASE STUDIES

The Tooth Body Connection

CS came to our office with specific orders from her healthcare provider. She wanted to have three teeth removed. X-rays confirmed two of the teeth were old root canal teeth that apparently had failed and re-infected. The third tooth was not showing any conventional signs of stress or infection and in every way appeared to be a healthy vital tooth. This presented a problem for the dentist. Should he remove a tooth based on an opinion that was non-dental? The patient had been advised that this tooth was on her lymph meridian.

Her primary reason for seeing this particular healthcare provider was his ability to find energy blockages by taking readings with electrodermal testing. CS had been diagnosed with Hodgkin's disease and had sought conventional treatment with no positive results. She was told that in order for **any** therapy to work, she would need to have the blockage cleared on that meridian. The most interesting thing happened after the removal of the tooth on the lymph meridian. The dentist sectioned the tooth in half to find the canals had calcified and that the tooth was in fact nonvital (dead).

Her healer's next step was to rid her of constant bladder pain that had been a chronic problem for her. Again, she was referred to our office with a diagnosis that a front tooth had been damaged, probably due to orthodontics, and would need to be extracted. The tooth was removed and a partial denture made to replace the tooth.

It has been almost three years since her surgeries and CS is proud to say that she is still here, doing well and that her bladder pain left with her tooth. CS states that she does not believe the removal of the tooth on the lymph meridian is the only reason for her success. She has been using many forms of alternative healing therapies and gives credit to all of them as a team. CS does say that the extraction of the tooth on the bladder meridian and the immediate relief she got from bladder pain was the most dramatic thing she experienced.

ANESTHETIC BLOCK AND CAVITATIONS

SB came to our office with a list of health maladies. For two years she had pain in her neck and shoulder. Her legs felt like pins were sticking in her and she had increasing difficulty with walking, at times even needing the use of a walker. Her complaints also included eye problems, fibrocystic breasts, stomach lesions from medications and headaches. She had been diagnosed as having Lupus by a conventional physician.

It was determined that a root canal on tooth #19 and several cavitation sites were focal points for some of her health problems. Her amalgams were replaced with composite restorations **at the patient's request**. The dentist decided to try an anesthetic block to confirm a connection between the teeth and the rest of the body. Within 30 seconds, after the injection of carbocaine, she began crying. Her leg had stopped hurting for the first time in over a year and her shoulder pains along with her headaches were gone. As the anesthetic wore off, the bottoms of her feet began tingling and pain started up her left leg. Three years have passed since her dental work was done. Her Lupus is in remission and SB enjoys the pain free life she has now. SB attributes her improved health to her dental work alone, as she has not changed her lifestyle at all.

HEAVY METALS

CM was referred to a dentist by a conventional physician that practices alternative health. The Dr's request was for the dentist to remove all amalgam from the patient due to high levels of mercury found in the patient. The health history was quite extensive; triple bypass surgery, high blood pressure, vertigo, ringing in his ears, depression, high blood sugar, headaches and flu like symptoms.

The doctor requesting the mercury removal did chelation therapy for heavy metal detoxification during the dental treatment to assist in the removal of the mercury from the body tissues. Within two weeks, following the mercury removal, the patient remarked that his blood pressure was the lowest it had ever been, his blood sugar had calmed down, his depression, ringing in his ears, headaches, vertigo and flu like symptoms were all gone.

A follow up two years after the removal shows the patient is still receiving chelation treatments with his doctor and he is enjoying good health. He states that he believes his mercury removal was instrumental in his improved health and acknowledges the chelation for its role in detoxing the mercury out of his system.

****

PW had been treating what she thought was Chronic Yeast Syndrome for years until a doctor suggested she might have heavy metal toxicity. Her symptoms were chronic fatigue, memory loss, poor concentration and depression. She went through blood compatibility testing to determine the best materials for her dental work. Her story is almost too remarkable to print. She stated that "within 24 hours she had 80% improvement in her fatigue, concentration and memory loss." She also wanted everyone to know that she "felt happy for the first time in six months." *I wonder if her depression was actually due to the depressive effect of silver?*

136

ROOT CANALS

KR had periodontal involvement of one mandibular molar. His mouth was in good periodontal shape with the exception of the lower left first molar. This tooth had bone loss of 7-8 mm around the tooth. X-ray revealed endodontic (root canal) treatment had been performed on this tooth, but no visible pathology was found. A deep curettage of the area was done under local anesthesia, to debride the area. The patient was given specific home care instructions about cleaning the area. The results were not achieved that had been hoped for, so KR was referred to a periodontist's office. They did surgery with bone augmentation. A year follow-up showed severe bone loss again. The patient opted to have the tooth removed. Exam of the tooth revealed a hair-line fracture. This fracture could have allowed toxins (anaerobic bacteria) to seep through the tooth and sit around the tooth causing bone destruction. Upon removal of the tooth, the periodontal ligament and diseased bone, the entire area has since filled in nicely with healthy bone. Had this area been left alone, it would have endangered the teeth on either side of it by destroying the bony support. KR felt frustrated with his old dental thinking, save the tooth at all costs. He spent over $4,000.00 trying to save a hopeless tooth.

GALVANISM

SJ was referred by a chiropractor that is very knowledgeable about the tooth body connection. She was 46 years of age at the time. Her complaints were long and chronic. His diagnosis was, incompatible dental materials were having effects on her health. He felt the need for her to have her dental work removed and replaced with something kinder and more compatible. Her existing dental work consisted of several types of restorations, done at different times with different metals. There were silver mercury amalgams, gold crowns, nickel crowns and some composite fillings with metal under them. The chiropractor used applied kinesiology to determine the best materials for her. Six months after complete removal, she made the following claims of improvement in her health.

Symptom
Percentage of Improvement

Unexplained Irritability	75%
Numbness and Tingling in Extremities	100%
Difficulty with Short Term Memory	90%
Irritable Bowel Syndrome	90%
Tremors of Hands and Feet	100%
Leg Cramps	100%
Ringing in Ears	50%
Frequent Heartburn	75%
Insomnia	90%
Burning Tongue	100%
Migraines	90%
Panic Attacks (screaming)	100%
Dizziness	100%

Mr. J.T. works at a job that puts him at risk of exposure to certain heavy metals. His employer requires hair analysis be done every year. J.T. has been working there since 1986. When he began working there he had never had any dental work done and was amalgam-free. His first test came back with a zero level of mercury.

In February of 1987 he now had dental insurance for the first time and made a visit to a local dentist. J.T. had a two surface, mercury amalgam placed in a lower right bicuspid. Nine months later, in November of 1987, his hair analysis came back with one *, denoting a trace of mercury was detected. In December of 1987 he had two more amalgams placed. The hair analysis done in November of 1988 showed 4 ****, this was a level the test results called, low normal. J.T. had no further dental work done from 1988-1991 and his test levels stayed at the 4 **** during that time period.

In March of 1992 J.T. was told a molar had a fracture line in it and would need a crown placed. This tooth was next to the first silver amalgam that was done. The filling touched the gold crown in between the two teeth. J.T. started complaining of a metal taste in his mouth about a week after the crown was cemented but his complaints fell on deaf ears. Three months later, the same tooth on the other side cracked, so it was crowned as well. This second crown was directly below a silver amalgam filling. The hair analysis done in November of 1992 came back with 40 *'s, placing him in a high toxicity level. This was a red flag to his employer, although they work with another heavy metal and not with any mercury. A physician was consulted and no answer could be found. *If you started having bladder problems after a front tooth was worked on or started having a funny taste in your mouth, who would think to call the dentist. Most conventional physicians are really not trained in this area.* In 1994 both crowns had endodontic (root canal) treatment. The dentist drilled through the top of the gold crown and when finished placed silver amalgam fillings in the holes. His mercury level had stayed 40 since the 1992 reading.

139

J.T. has been doing a lot of research on his own and decided, after reading a book *"It's All in your Head"* by Dr. Hal Huggins DDS, that his problem might be dental related. *Now, I would like to stress that the dentist he was seeing, is very competent as a conventional dentist. Every procedure was done following the standard protocol that almost every dentist trained today follows.*

It took me a while to put the puzzle together, of dates dental work was done, and dates the test results came back. After seeing the dates and the test results, it was pretty evident that J.T. was experiencing galvanism. The gold crown touching the amalgam had really high current readings. The gold crown and the silver amalgam next to it were both severely pitted due to the corrosion of the galvanic reaction. This reaction caused the mercury to leach out at incredible levels.

The dental work was replaced with porcelain crowns and composite (plastic) fillings. J.T. went through several DMPS challenges and is at the low trace level now.

PERSONAL COMMENT

My hope is that after reading this you will be better equipped to find a dentist that will adhere to the oath all Dr's take "First do no harm." Feel justified in asking questions about the office you are considering. Will they honor your requests or make fun of you? Here are some sample questions.

Does your office use mercury silver or amalgam fillings?
If you want a Biological dentist the correct answer will be - NO!

Do you know how to remove amalgams safely?
If they answer "What do you mean"? then they don't know.

Do you use a nose piece and a rubber dam during amalgam removal?
Correct answer- Yes

Do you use an amalgameter to determine the correct sequence of removal?
Correct answer- Yes

Does your office have a way of testing compatibility?
Correct answer- Yes

Does your office work with a physician, osteopath or chiropractor for the purposes of detoxing?
They should be able to refer you to several offices..

What kind of continuing education does the dentist attend? How often?

Dentistry is changing for the better at an incredible pace. Make sure they are keeping abreast.

How are the instruments sterilized?

Answer- Heat sterilization and chemical sterilization.

Realize that you may find many differences between practitioners. The very strict biological dental office may not do root canals or implants. They may not use any fluoride pastes or rinses. The staff may not wear hair sprays or perfumes that would bother a chemically sensitive patient. There may be higher speed suctions than found in the usual dental office. They may use the low speed handpieces more often. They may have specialized air filters and water filters.

You have a **right to know**. Any office that is hesitant to answer is not a match for you. When my son was four, he broke the back of a baby molar. I took him to a children's dentist in our area. After the exam of the tooth, the dentist's recommendation was a pulpectomy (baby root canal) and a stainless steel crown. He made that choice based on two facts 1) that I had insurance that would not pay for white fillings and 2) the skill needed to place a white filling in a small, wet area like a child's mouth is extremely difficult. Now granted, I had experience enough to know that the nerve was not involved and that the area could be restored with a filling. After expressing my views and opinions, my only comment was, "If you do not have the skills necessary to place the requested material, I will seek treatment elsewhere." I challenged him to give it his best effort. My son has a great filling and we now have a new referral source for our younger patients.

In Germany, they worded laws to protect the patient. If the dentist places materials in a patient that later cause health problems for the patient, the dentist is held accountable. If you were a German dentist would you use amalgams? Remember that the Germans are far beyond us in the belief of the meridians and the teeth connecting with the rest of the body.

We all want good health. Sometimes we take it for granted until we lose it. Find a good biological dentist for your family. Sure, he will be more expensive! Remember he uses higher quality materials. For example, the office I am in now has full spectrum lighting in every bulb! We have a heavy duty water filter on the water lines and then individual bacterial filters on each drill and water syringe. Most people are clueless to the water woes, so why would a dentist care? It just goes in your mouth! There are air purifying filtration systems and a high pressure vacuum to remove vapors. Most dentists use a drill over and over until it gets dull. Mind you they do sterilize it between patients. Our office uses one per patient and sometimes more may be used for that one person. As the drill dulls, it heats the tooth. Heating the tooth may cause nerve damage and slowly kill the tooth. We use air abrasion (drill-less therapy) to remove decay whenever possible. This process uses a spray of powder like a miniature sandblaster to remove decay without heating the tooth. When amalgams are being removed, our patients have oxygen masks placed on their nose to prevent inhalation of the toxic mercury fumes. We also use rubber dams on the teeth to prevent any dust generated from the removal of mercury filling from going into the mouth and being swallowed. Rubber dams are not used by most dentists because they are difficult to put on, are time consuming and are too expensive for them to bother with. The question is, "Are these unnecessary expenses to incur higher fees?" The answer is, No. They are for your health and the health of those working in that environment.

I get questioned about insurance all the time. Why won't my insurance pay for the more expensive composite filling? They will only pay for the cheaper silver filling. My answer is a question, "Are they really interested in your health or the economic health of their company?". Another statement I hear is, "I only want what my insurance will pay for." Think of your health insurance, they won't pay for vitamins to prevent you from getting sick, but they will pay for expensive drugs once you do get sick. They won't pay for chelation therapy to improve circulation to a diabetic's leg, but they will pay for the amputation! Now, do you really want what insurance will pay for? Your insurance is not interested in your health, calling it health insurance is a joke; it is sick insurance; it only pays when you are sick.

My life has taken me from a conventional dental field beginning in 1975 into a medical career and back to dentistry; but this time with a tooth body connection. The experience has been extremely rewarding and satisfying. I have been on an uncharted quest with my final destination yet unknown, but more exciting than most people's I'm sure. I currently teach courses on electro-dermal testing as it pertains to dentistry. This involves a good working knowledge of the body, the teeth, and the acupuncture points. As the future brings more people to seek alternatives to the conventional, I'll be there!

[1]Voll R. *Verification of acupuncture by means of electroacupuncture by Voll*. Am J Acupuncture 1977; 6: 5-15

[2]Berstein M: *Double blind food challenge in diagnosis of food sensitivity in the adult*. J. Clin. Immunology 1974; 54 : 165

[3]Voll R. : *Twenty years of electroacupuncture diagnosis in Germany. A progress report*. Am. J. Acupuncture 1975; 3 (19) : 7-17

[4]Tiller, W.A. : *What do electrodermal diagnostic acupuncture instruments really measure?* Amer. J. Acupuncture Vol. 15, No. 1 March 1987, pp 15-23.

[5]Meinig,G.E., : Root Canal Cover Up Bion publishing, Ojion, Calif. 1994, second edition

[6]Huggins, H.A., It's All In Your Head - Toxic Element Research Foundation Colorado Springs, Co 1985

[7]Skinner, E. W., and Phillips, R. and W., ' *The science of dental materials*' ; sixth edition, Philadelphia: W. B. Saunders Co. 1969, 303 and 332.

[8]Sharma and Obersteiner ; *Metals and Neurotoxic Effects; Cytotoxicity of Selected Compounds on Chick Ganglia Cultures*; J. of Comparative Pathology; Vol 91, 235-244, 1981.

[9]Clarkson, T.W.; Friberg, L.; Hursch, J. and Nylander, M. In: Biological Monitoring of Toxic Metals, Plenum Press, N.Y. Feb 1988.

[10]Nylander, Magnus; Friberg Lars; Lind Birger: " *Mercury Concentrations in Human Brain and Kidneys in Relation to Exposure from Dental Amalgam Filling*": Swed. Dent. J. 11: 179-187, 1987.

[11]Wenstrup, D, Ehmann, W.D. and Markesbery, W.R., *Brain Res.*, 1990, 533, 125-31.

[12]Summers, A. O. et al, *Antimicrob. Agents and Chemother.*, 1993, 37, 825-34.

[13]Amer Academy of Dental Science, ' *A history of dental and oral science in America'*; Philadelphia: Samuel White, 1876.

[14]Bremmer, D.K., ' *The Story of Dentistry'*, revised third edition, Brooklyn: Dental Items of Interest Publishing, 1954.

[15]Ring M., ' *Dentistry, an Illustrated History'*, New York: Harryu N. Abrams, 1985

[16]Social Styrelsen (Sweden, Social Welfare and Health Administration), Press Release, 28th August 1992.

[17]Bundesquesundheitsamt (German Ministry of Health), Letter to Pharmaceutical companies, 29th Jan Artezeitung (Physician's Daily), 3rd March 1992.

[18]Austrian Minister of Health, '*Austria to be Amalgam Free'* , FDI Dental World, March/ April 1993, 6.

[19]Whitaker, J., ' *Other Countries Ban Mercury'* J. Health and

Healing April 1996 pg. 2.

[20]Ziff, S., Silver Dental Fillings- The Toxic Time Bomb, Aurora Press, New York, N. Y. 1984, 1986.

[21]Brake, M. ' Defense Against Mystery Syndromes' Revealing the Mystery of "Silver" Fillings. DAMS, Albuquerque, N.M. 1993.

[22]Eggleston, David, D.D.S. ; *Effect of Dental Amalgam and Nickel Alloys of T- Lymphocytes*: J. Prosthetic Dentistry, Vol 51, No 5; 617-623, May 1984.

[23]Huggins, Hal, It's All In Your Head, Toxic Element Research Foundation, Colorado Springs, Co 1985.

[24]Goldberg, Burton 'Alternative medicine' Future Medicine Publishing, Fife, Washington, 1994 pg 80-95.

[25]Gosselin, R., M.D., Ph. D. : Smith, R., Ph. D. ; and Hodge, H., Ph.D., D.S.C.; Clinical Toxicology of Commercial Products, Fifth edition.

[26]Solomon, H.A., and M. C. Reinhard " *Electric Phenomena from Dental Materials*" Dental Survey, 9:23 (Jan 1933)

[27]Schoonover, I.C., and W. Sounder. "Corrosion of Dental Alloys." Journal of American Dental Association, 28 (part 2), 1278, 1941.

[28]Schriever, W., and L. E. Diamond, "*Electromotive Forces and Electric Currents Caused by Metallic Dental Fillings.*" Journal of Dental Research, 18: 205 (1938).

[29]Proceedings of the International Conference on Biocompatibility of Materials, November 1988, in publication currently by Life Sciences Press, Tacoma, Wa.

[30]Eggleston, David, D.D.S.; *Effect of Dental Amalgam and Nickel Alloys of T- Lymphocytes*: J Prosthetic Dentistry, Vol, 51, No 5; 617-623, May 1984.

[31]Lippmann, A. " *Disorders Caused by Electrical Discharges in the Mouth with Artificial Dentures*." Deutsche Med. Wchnschr., 56: 1394 (1930).

[32]Becker, R. O., M. D., *Cross Currents, The Promise of Electro- Medicine, The Perils of Electro-Pollution*, Los Angeles, ZJeremy P. Tarcher, Inc. 1990.

[33]Becker, R. O., M. D.; and Selden, G. *'The Body Electric; Electromagnetism and the Foundation of Life'*, New York: William Morrow and Company, 1985.

[34]Gosau, H.D.; *'Focus Caused Iatrogenic Damages: Pathologic Connections of So Called Mouth Currents.'* J. Academy for Biocybernetic Total Medicine pg 52-59, 1992.

[35]Meinig: Root Canal Cover Up, Bion Publishing, Ojai Calif, 1994, 2nd edition.

[36]Cook, D. L., D.D.S., 10971 Clinic Road, Suring Wi., Center for Bio-Energetic Medicine.

[37]Goldberg, Burton 'Alternative Medicine' Future Medicine

Publishing, Fife, Washington, 1994, pg 80-95.

[38]Proceedings of the International Conference on Biocompatibility of Materials, Nov 1988, in publication currently by Life Sciences Press, Tacoma, Wa.

[39]Landermann, Andy, D.D.S., N.D., 650 4th Street, Santa Rosa, Calif.

Other Resources

The International DAMS (Dental Amalgam Mercury Survivors)
800-311-6265

American Academy of Biological Dentistry
831-659-5385

International Academy of Oral Medical Toxicology (IAOMT)
407-298-2450

Environmental Dental Association
800-388-8124

Capital University of Integrative Medicine
202-338-4646

Tooth and Gum (Mouthwash and Toothpaste)
Dental Herb Company, Inc
800-747-Herb

Clifford Consulting and Research (Compatibility)
719-550-0008

Peak Energy Performance (Hal Huggins)
800-331-2303

Institute for Health Realities- (Sam Queen)
719-598-4968

Transformation Enzymes (Enzymes)
800-777-1474

CAVITAT (Bone Density Imaging)
303-755-2688
Affinity Labeling Technology (TOPAZ testing)
606-388-9445
www.altcorp.com

BioMeridian (Meridian Stress Assessment)
801-501-7517

Extended Health (Oral Chelation)
800-300-6712

Energetix (Opening the Channels and Homeopathics)
800-990-7085
www.goenergetix.com

Metal Free (Oral Chelation)
877-804-3258
www.bodyhealth.com

Natural Lighting (Full Spectrum Lights)
www.naturallighting.com
1-888-900-6830

Deseret Biological (Homeopathics and Instapoint program)
800-827-9529

Energique (Homeopathics)
800-869-8078

Rocky Mountain (Anodyne Therapy)
303-699-8700
rmht@rockymountainhealth.com

Suggested Reading

Beyond Amalgam by Susan Stockton, Natur's Publishing, Ltd (941) 426-1929

Fluoride the Aging Factor by Dr John Yiamouyiannis Health Action Press, 6439 Taggart Road, Delaware, Ohio 43015

Are Your Dental Fillings Poisoning You? by Guy S. Fasciana, D.M.D. Keats Publishing, New Canaan, Connecticut

Dentistry Without Mercury by Sam Ziff and Michael Ziff, D.D.S Bio-Probe, Inc P.O. Box 608010, Orlando, Fl 32860

Alternative Medicine the Definitive Guide by the Goldberg Group Future Medicine Publishing, Inc, 5009 Pacific Hwy. E. Suite 6, Fife, Washington 98424

How To Save Your Teeth by David Kennedy D.D.S. Health Action Press, 6439 Taggart Road, Delaware, Ohio 43015

Defense Against Mystery Syndromes by DAMS 505-888-0111

Uniformed Consent by Hal Huggins D.D.S., and Thomas Levy M.D. Hampton Roads Publishing Company, Inc 800-766-8009

Mercury Poisoning from Dental Amalgams by Patrick Stortebecker, M.D., Ph.D. Bio-Probe, Inc, P.O. Box 58010, Orlando, FL 32858

Root Canal Cover Up by George Meinig D.D.S., F.A.C.D. Bion Publishing Ojai, California

Cure for All Diseases by Hulda Clark, PhD, N.D. 1-800-231-1776

Tooth Truth by Frank Jerome, D.D.S. 1-800-231-1776

Toxic Time Bomb by Sam Ziff Aurora Press P.O. Box 573, Santa Fe, N.M. 87504

The Missing Link by Micharl F. Ziff,D.D.S. and Sam Ziff Bio-Probe, Inc P.O. Box 608010 Orlando, FL 32860

The Healing Power of Enzymes by DicQie Fuller , Ph.D., D.Sc. Forbes Custom Publishing ISBN 0-8281-1289-4

ORDER BLANK

Please mail me _____ copies of "Let the Tooth Be Known" to the following address; enclosed is my check/money order/charge card number for the total: Holistic Health Alternatives 17222 Red Oak Drive Suite 101 Houston, Texas 77090.

____copies @ $22.00 each. $22.00 x ___ = _____

____ 7.25% state sales tax (Texas residents only)
$1.59 ea. x ___ = _____

____ Dental Meridian Charts Laminated $25.00 each

Total .... = _____

Name _____

Address _____

City _____

State _____ Zip _____

OUR WEB ADDRESS IS
www.drdawn.net